Packet Video

Modeling and Signal Processing

For a complete listing of the *Artech House Telecommunications Library*, turn to the back of this book

Packet Video

Modeling and Signal Processing

Naohisa Ohta

Artech House
Boston • London

Library of Congress Cataloging-in-Publication Data

Ohta, Naohisa.
Packet video: modeling and signal processing / Naohisa Ohta.
Includes bibliographical references and index.
ISBN 0-89006-519-5
1. Image transmission. 2. Image processing. 3. Packet switching (Data transmission).
4. Digital communications. I. Title.
TK5105.2.O37   1994   93-38080
621.388—dc20   CIP

British Library Cataloguing in Publication Data

A catalogue record for this book is available from the British Library.

© 1994 ARTECH HOUSE, INC.
685 Canton Street
Norwood, MA 02062

International Standard Book Number: 0-89006-519-5
Library of Congress Catalog Card Number: TK5105.2.O37

10 9 8 7 6 5 4 3 2 1

To Yumiko and Natsuki

Contents

Preface

Packet video means transmitting packetized video signals in real time. Although packet transmission of digital data has a long history, packet video is a new concept. The digitalization of visual media and telecommunication networks, supported by the advance of VLSI signal processing technologies, has given birth to the packet video concept. In the late 1980s, in the initial research and development stages of *Integrated Services Digital Network* (ISDN), the concept of packet voice transmission had been proposed and investigated. However, its protocol used a complex error handling scheme and limited transmission speeds to several tens of kilobits per second. In the discussion of future broadband ISDN (B-ISDN), how to flexibly achieve the much higher rates required for the transmission of broadband signals has become a central technical issue. Asynchronous transfer mode (ATM) was proposed to achieve both high-speed transmission and flexibility. A short, fixed-length packet format and a very simple error handling scheme were employed for this reason. Thus, the ATM technology enables us to transmit real-time video signals at variable bit rates in the form of packets. At the same time, advances in digital signal processing and VLSI technology make it possible to implement sophisticated image processing algorithms in real time using compact hardware. Under these circumstances, much effort has been spent on researching packet video transmission for future visual communications.

In order to achieve packet video in B-ISDN environments, a variety of advanced technologies are indispensable: compression algorithms, characterization of video signals, video signal processing, stochastic analysis, and network protocol designs. They are new issues because there has not been a close technological connection between traditional visual media and digital communications networks.

This book covers a number of the technological issues associated with packet video and introduces results from the last five years of research in this field with emphasis on the modeling and signal processing of video signals. The discussions center on the results of research performed by the author's group related to the modeling of video signals, variable-rate video coding, and packet loss protection and recovery techniques. This book is also intended to provide comprehensive discussions on the framework of the technological issues, targeting readers who want a brief understanding of packet video technologies.

A brief overview of this book is as follows. Chapter 1 is the introduction of this book and describes the background of packet video. Chapter 2 covers the current state of digital communications networks, including the movement toward standardization of B-ISDN, centering on ATM technology. We discuss briefly the relationship between the network and various services that use visual media transmitted over B-ISDN. This chapter can be skipped by readers with a certain degree of knowledge of digital communications networks. Chapters 3 and 4 cover the characteristics of digital video information sources. We present measurement results on the variable-rate and burst characteristics of various types of image sources and investigations into source models based on those results. Chapter 5 describes the basic structure of variable-rate encoding, improved image quality achievable with variable-rate encoding, measures to prevent quality degradation in the face of information loss, a variety of layered encoding algorithms, and examples of encoding schemes in actual use. Chapter 6 considers packet loss protection and recovery techniques in packet video transmission. The technologies used at the network and the user levels are described. The most promising technology based on the layered coding scheme is discussed. Chapter 7 introduces the latest discussions on user/network interfacing technologies associated with packet video transmission.

Few extant texts have covered these technological issues in any systematic manner because this is a very young field. The objective of this book is to present the framework results and to provide a starting point for readers who want a systematic review of packet video technologies.

Acknowledgments

The author is indebted to many friends and colleagues for their stimulating interaction and discussion of the topics in this book. Deserving of special mention is Mitsuru Nomura, who was a member of the author's group and derived many of the results described in Chapters 3–5. The author also thanks Tetsurou Fujii, Junji Suzuki, and Sadayasu Ono for their comments and suggestions on the subject. Other colleagues who have contributed to the contents in this book include Naoaki Yamanaka, Ken-Ichi Sato, and Youichi Sato. The author would like to thank Mark Garrett and Helmut Heeke for their contribution of the latest results on packet video.

The author also would like to thank Tetsuya Miki, Tomonori Aoyama, and Haruo Yamaguchi of NTT for their help and support in the course of research and writing this book.

In addition, many thanks to Bonnie Sullivan for her excellent help in translation and Michael Blackburn for his correction of the final manuscript.

Special thanks go to Mark Walsh of Artech House for his commitment to this book and to Pamela Ahl and Lisa Tomasello for their editorial assistance.

Finally, the author wishes to acknowledge the individuals and organizations cited in the captions of numerous figures and tables in this book for their permission to use said material.

Chapter 1
Introduction

1.1 VISUAL MEDIA AND COMMUNICATION

Communication mediated by visual media has an extremely long history. Cave drawings from prehistoric times can be considered one of the earliest uses of these kinds of media, which we refer to here as "visual media." Media such as these can speak to us across the ages. As time progressed, and it became possible to print or display pictures and characters on paper or a screen, and as commercial distribution systems developed, these types of media were used for communication without regard for distance, that is, telecommunication. With the advent of television, a medium was born that could transmit moving pictures in real time directly into the homes of the recipients.

Television mainly uses a broadcast format to realize one-way communication to a large number of nonspecific recipients. By comparison, the telephone provides a one-to-one communications system, and voice communication has become the focus of contemporary electronic communications. In fact, today's enormous global communications network is organized around the telephone circuit, a channel that passes voice bandwidth signals as its basic unit. In recent years, this facility has come to be used to transmit images of documents, and currently, this application accounts for much of the traffic on telephone circuits, which were originally intended for voice communications. Of course, we are referring to facsimile, or fax, communication.

Fax is the first visual media to gain wide acceptance for use across communications networks. However, in its present form, fax is still a rather strange combination of digital and analog technologies. As the reader probably knows, a document transmitted by fax has been decomposed into only black and white pixels, and redundancy compression has been performed. This intrinsically digital information is then transmitted by modulating the communication circuit's analog signal, and the transmission speed is therefore limited by the frequency bandwidth of the circuit.

At the current time, digitalization of the communications system is progressing, and 64-Kbps digital circuits based on the Integrated Services Digital Network (ISDN) concept are becoming available. At the same time, the digitalization of all types of visual media is progressing rapidly. We can finally see the point in the near future at which integrated, digital visual communications (both media and communications totally digital) will be available.

1.2 DIGITALIZATION OF MEDIA AND COMMUNICATIONS

1.2.1 Visual Media

Many types of visual media, including television (broadcast and cable TV), video cassette, laser disk, CD-ROM, and commercial cinema are currently in use. Until recently, nearly all visual media were both stored and transmitted as analog signals. However, progress in digital storage technologies, such as magnetic disk, cartridge tape, and CD-ROM for computers and engineering workstations, has proceeded at an astounding pace. Current technology supports 2 GB of storage on a compact hard disk or 1 GB on an 8-mm magnetic tape. Because they are stable and relatively immune to deterioration, visual media based on digital signals can be replayed with very high quality. Although large digital memories are, in general, required to process these signals, projected advances in very-large-scale integration (VLSI) technology will shortly provide adequate memory speed and size. In short, signal processing of digital visual media will become very easy.

A point to keep in mind when considering the digitalization of visual media is that digitalization of visual media is proceeding independently of that of the communications channel. Furthermore, as we see in the latest multimedia advances, visual media are being integrated with other media. While we do not discuss this realm in detail here, the reader will surely recognize the phenomenon we are referring to if we interject a few buzzwords from currently active new media areas: digital video interactive (DVI), desktop publishing (DTP), digital high-definition television (HDTV), and the hypermedia personal computer [1]. For example, the monitor screens of workstation-class computers have already exceeded the quality of normal television, and there are already applications in which a video signal is displayed in a portion of the workstation screen. Visual media themselves are becoming digitalized in this manner, and although package media such as compact disks are at the center of this trend, it is clear that requirements for the transmission of these digital signals over communications networks will follow. (See Figure 1.1.)

1.2.2 Network Technology

Communications network technology is also developing rapidly. The 3.4-kHz bandwidth analog line, centered on providing telephone service, is giving way to the 64-Kbps digital line and the even higher speed 1.5-Mbps line, and we are just beginning to see high-speed digital lines (several tens of Mbps), based on optical fiber technology, at a reasonable price. These services are made possible by the combination of high-speed transmission

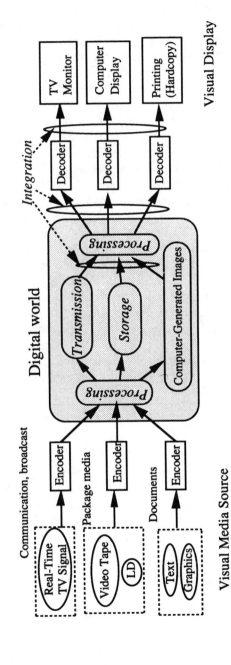

Figure 1.1 Visual media digitalization.

technology based on optical fibers, high-speed circuit technology (for fast digital data processing), and high-speed switching technology. The network does not merely provide a high-speed "pipe," but is also beginning to provide new functionality that alters the ways in which it can be used. For example, in asynchronous transfer mode (ATM), information is divided into fixed-length packets that are labeled and transmitted at high speed [2–4]. This scheme provides far more freedom in terms of transmission rate than the traditional transfer modes, in which fixed channeles are assigned. In the age of this kind of technology, it will be possible to transmit over the communications networks not only the fax that we see in widespread use today, but also higher quality images and even full motion video [5–7]. As the flexibility of the network increases, it will become possible to realize many new forms of communication. Some businesses are already using teleconferencing, in which video and voice are transmitted simultaneously in both directions, as a means to overcome distances. In fact, teleconferencing can be considered the first multimedia communications application. While it is difficult to determine exactly the image quality required for satisfactory teleconferencing, current systems use a transmission bandwidth of between some small multiple of 64 Kbps and 2 Mbps.

For example, CCITT H.261 advances a video encoding scheme using transmission speeds from 64 Kbps to 2 Mbps. H.261 is intended for use principally with bidirectional visual media, such as teleconferencing and video telephone [8,9]. The Moving Picture Experts Group (MPEG) is an example of progress toward standardization of an encoding method for the storage of even higher quality images [10]. MPEG's first target for standardization, MPEG-I (codified in the 1992 draft international standard), was set at the rate of approximately 1.5 Mbps, including the audio signal. The next step, called MPEG-II, is to standardize rates up to 10 Mbps using currently (1993) available algorithms. The current trend in visual communications in terms of network digitalization is shown in Figure 1.2.

1.2.3 Digital Signal Processing

To transmit visual media based on analog technology over a digital network, obviously the data must first be digitized and transferred to the network as a digital data sequence. To use a given communication line efficiently, transmitting information as cheaply as possible but with the highest quality possible, the digitized information must first be processed to remove redundancy. Advances in the basic technologies of digital signal processing and VLSI technology are necessary before this type of processing can become feasible.

Progress in VLSI technology has brought us compact, low-cost components for terminal I/O, redundancy compression encoding, and signal processing elements within the network itself. The trend toward more compact, lower price terminal equipment will have its largest impact on visual media communications. While there are no consumers who have installed mainframe-class computers in their homes, many do already own

Visual Media

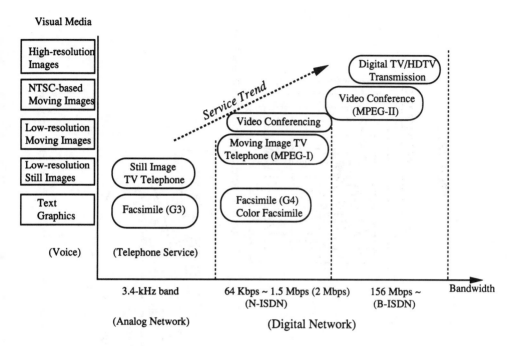

Figure 1.2 Network digitalization and visual media.

a personal computer. The contemporary personal computer has computational power comparable to that of early large-scale mainframes, yet takes up less than one percent of the space. Due to high line use fees and large terminal size, the TV telephone seen in early science fiction movies did not come into common use, despite successful technology demonstrations. However, in the last two or three years, visual telephones based on analog telephone lines and TV telephones using 64-Kbps digital circuits have been commercially introduced. But in an ironic twist, image quality is now seen as a problem, and this generation of the technology does not seem destined to succeed.

1.3 THE DEVELOPMENT OF PACKET VIDEO

The progress of digitalization of visual media and telecommunication networks, supported by the advance of VLSI signal processing technologies, has given birth to the packet video concept. *Packet video* means transmitting digitized and packetized video signals in real time. (See Figure 1.3.)

Transmission of packetized broadband signals in real time could never be realized in the analog world. At the beginning of ISDN research and development, the concept of packet voice transmission had been proposed and investigated [11,12]. The primary purpose of packet voice transmission was to utilize finite communications capacity effi-

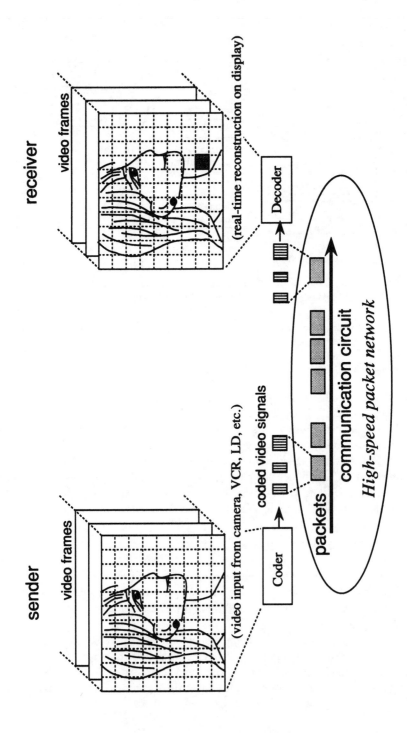

Figure 1.3 The concept of packet video transmission. (Example: Transmission between the center and a terminal in video distribution services or between multimedia terminals, etc.)

ciently by sending only significant voice signals in the form of packets. The protocol available for packet voice was X.25, which was developed originally for data transmission [13]. Its complex error handling scheme limited transmission speeds to several tens of kilobits per second.

In the discussion of future Broadband Integrated Services Digital Networks (B-ISDNs), how to expand flexibility to the higher rates required for transmission of broadband signals has become a central technical issue. As mentioned in the previous section, ATM was proposed to achieve both high-speed transmission and flexibility. A short, fixed-length packet format and a very simple error handling scheme was employed for this reason. Thus, the ATM technology enables us to transmit real-time video signals at variable bit rates in the form of packets. High-speed LAN technologies have also made it possible to provide high-speed, flexible computer communications. At the same time, advances in digital signal processing and VLSI technology make it possible to implement sophisticated image processing algorithms in real time and with compact hardware. Under these circumstances, much effort has been spent on research into packet video transmission for the future visual communications. (See Figure 1.4.)

Because video signal transmission requires much higher bit rates than voice signals, the primary purpose of packet video is to achieve efficient video transmission by utilizing statistical packet multiplexing. Furthermore, packet video transmission should provide a *higher quality of services*, in terms of the service flexibility, rate variability, and constant

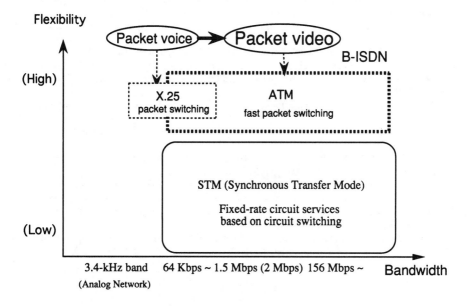

Figure 1.4 Development of the packet video concept.

video quality achievable with variable-rate transmission [14]. It is also noteworthy that packet video will support multimedia transmission.

We see that a number of technological issues will have to be addressed before B-ISDNs can be utilized for packet video and for transmitting a variety of visual media efficiently and in large volume. They are new issues because this close technological connection between traditional visual media and digital communications networks did not previously exist. For example, it is very important for network designers to know the characteristics of variable-rate video signals, but the statistics of video signals coded with sophisticated coding schemes have not been well understood. Video encoding schemes and user/network interfaces must also be designed with an awareness of packet video in order to achieve efficient, high-quality services. This book explores the technological issues inherent in packet video. It also provides a starting point for readers who want a brief review of packet video technologies, with emphasis on the modeling and signal processing of video signals.

REFERENCES

[1] Fox, E. A., "Advances in Interactive Digital Multimedia Systems," *Computer*, Vol. 24, No. 10, 1991, pp. 9–21.

[2] Minzer, S. E., "Broadband ISDN and Asynchronous Transfer Mode (ATM)," *IEEE Communications Magazine*, Vol. 27, No. 9, Sept. 1989, pp. 17–24.

[3] Day, A., "International Standardization of BISDN," *The Magazine of Lightwave Telecommunication Systems*, Vol. 2, No. 3, 1991, pp. 13–20.

[4] Kawarasaki, M., and Jabbari, B., "B-ISDN Architecture and Protocol," *IEEE Journal on Selected Areas in Communications*, Vol. 9, No. 9, Dec. 1991, pp. 1405–1415.

[5] Turner, J. S., "New Direction in Communications," in Proc., *Zurich Seminar*, 1986, p.35.

[6] Turner, J. S., "Fast Packet Switching and Visual Communication," *Multimedia '89*, Ottawa, April 1989.

[7] Ohta, N., et al., "Video Distribution on ATM-Based Optical Ring Networks," *Proc. ICC '90*, April 1990, pp. 976–980.

[8] Okubo, S., "Video CODEC Standardization in CCITT Study Group XV," *Image Communication*, Vol. 1, No. 1, 1989, pp. 45–54.

[9] Liou, M., "Overview of the p × 64 Kbps Coding Standard," *Communications of the ACM*, Vol. 34, No. 4, Apr. 1991, pp. 59–63.

[10] LeGall, D., "MPEG: A Video Compression Standard for Multimedia Applications," *Communications of the ACM*, Vol. 34, No. 4, Apr. 1991, pp. 46–58.

[11] Stern, T. E., "A Queuing Analysis of Packet Voice," *Proc. IEEE GLOBECOM '83*, Dec. 1983, pp. 71–76.

[12] Daigle, J. N., and Langford, J. D., "Models of Analysis of Packet Voice Communications Systems," *IEEE Journal on Selected Areas in Communications*, Vol. SAC-4, Sept. 1986, pp. 847–855.

[13] CCITT *Blue Book*, Recommendations X.1-X.32, 1989.

[14] Nomura, M., Fujii, T., Ohta, N., "Basic Characteristics of Variable Rate Video Coding in ATM Environment," *IEEE Journal on Selected Areas in Communications*, Vol. 7, No. 5, June 1989, pp. 752–760.

Chapter 2
B-ISDN and Visual Communications

2.1 INTRODUCTION

This chapter provides an introduction to the basic features and characteristics of communications networks that will be required for visual communications. First, we describe the structure and features of the digital communications networks currently under development and, in particular, compare the features of synchronous transfer mode (STM) and asynchronous transfer mode (ATM) networks. Then, we discuss the features of the visual communications services that will be provided over these digital communications networks. Finally, we discuss the basic ideas behind the variable rate transmission of image and video signals, and the impact of that technology.

2.2 THE DIGITAL NETWORK HIERARCHY

2.2.1 The Inception of Digitalization

The earliest targets towards the digitalization of public networks were the lines used for transmission of pulse code modulation (PCM) encoded digital voice signals. In the latter half of the 1960s, 24-circuit PCM multiplexing was introduced in North America and Japan; 30-circuit PCM multiplexing was introduced in Europe at about the same time. The voice encoding schemes used in these systems were established as the G.711 recommendations of the International Telegraph and Telephone Consultative Committee (CCITT) [1]. In both these systems, a single voice line is encoded at 64 Kbps. This 64-Kbps rate is based on sampling the voice signal at 8 kHz and taking an 8b nonlinear quantization of each sample, that is, 64 Kbps is 8b per sample times 8K samples per second [2]. This 64-Kbps rate became the basic unit of the digital hierarchy. However, this technology was not introduced in a form that allowed the user direct access to a 64-Kbps circuit. Initially, only transmission between central offices in metropolitan areas was digitalized. (This is known in North America as the T1 carrier system.) The motivation for this was the reduction of intermediate transmission costs by circuit multiplexing. While the specific circumstances differed from one country to another, digital transmission was introduced thereafter in various media, including coaxial cable, microwave transmission, and optical fiber technologies. Even as digitalization of the network proceeded, with circuits and switching equipment within the network being converted to digital operation, the traditional 3.4-kHz analog circuit continued to be the only interface offered to the end user.

At the same time that the telephone network was switching over to digital technology, the rapid development and growth of the computer field was increasing recognition of the necessity of digital networks for data communications. Standards for such networks, the *X series recommendations*, were developed in the latter half of the 1960s. These standards can be broadly categorized into circuit-switching and packet-switching schemes [3]. These schemes specified special interfaces, with several speed classes, for connecting data terminals onto the network. However, at first there was no demand for data communications over isolated digital networks. In actuality, most digital communication was carried out over public or private telephone lines using modems.

Thus public networks did not begin to offer digital lines to general users until digitalization had proceeded as far as the subscriber line. Integrated Services Digital Network (ISDN) service, based on 64-Kbps lines, was first introduced in the late 1980s [4]. In fact, some 20 years passed before digitalization, beginning with transmission circuits, finally began to extend to services. The current ISDN service, based on 64-Kbps circuits, is expected to give way to even higher speed broadband ISDN. When the two must be distinguished, the former is referred to as N-ISDN (for *narrowband* ISDN), and the latter as B-ISDN (for *broadband* ISDN).

The development in the computer field that is exerting the greatest influence on communications networks is the growth of local-area network (LAN) technology. LANs are mainly constructed for communications between computers in a single workplace, and LAN technology has developed very rapidly since the spread of engineering workstations in the 1980s. Ethernet, which provides a 10-Mbps transfer rate over coaxial cable, is a representative LAN technology [5]. While LANs developed independently of the public networks, public networks are the vehicle by which multiple LANs are connected. In essence, the user constructs an independent private network by connecting the user's LAN to one or more leased lines.

Figure 2.1 shows developments and expected trends in network digitalization.

2.2.2 Synchronous Digital Networks

The critical issue for efficient transmission of multiple lines, as well as for efficient circuit switching, is the method used for multiplexing the lines. The primary purpose of early network digitalization was to lower transmission costs, and multiplexing methods were

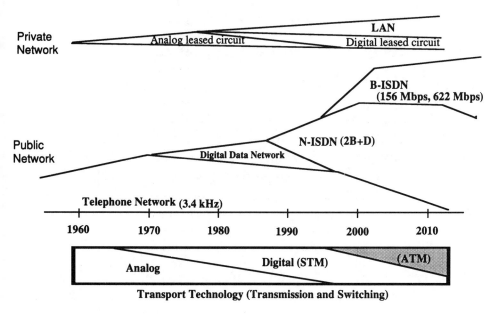

Figure 2.1 The digitalization of networks.

evaluated according to the number of pulses they could jam into transmission lines. "Stuff" became the predominant multiplexing method in early digital transmission. In the stuff method, digital signals (pulse sequences) multiplexed over multiple circuits are supposed to have rates that differ only slightly, and the transmission rate is adjusted by insertion and deletion of "stuffing" pulses to force a fixed rate. The advantage of the stuff scheme is that it allows multiple lines to be efficiently multiplexed without requiring high-stability clock synchronization. However, its flexibility with respect to the multiplexing hierarchy and in regard to switching circuits over various levels is limited. For example, multiplexing from low speeds to high speeds must be performed one level at a time. On the other hand, if a high-stability clock is supplied over the network, it becomes possible to synchronize all signal pulse sequences, and extremely flexible schemes that support jump-multiplexing and electronic circuit switching become possible. These are known as synchronous multiplexing schemes.

Traditionally, interfaces between layers in the digital hierarchy have been asynchronous, and there were three main groups at the international level. (Figure 2.2(a).) There is an increasing awareness that this situation is not desirable from the standpoints of expanding the scale of future networks to a global scale and supporting new services, especially B-ISDN. In 1988, as a result of great efforts within the CCITT, the network node interface (NNI), a unified world synchronous multiplexing interface, was standardized [6]. As shown in Figure 2.2(b), Synchronous Digital Hierarchy (SDH) is a unified world hierarchy with a base speed of about 156 Mbps; it subsumes group 1 (1.5 Mbps in North

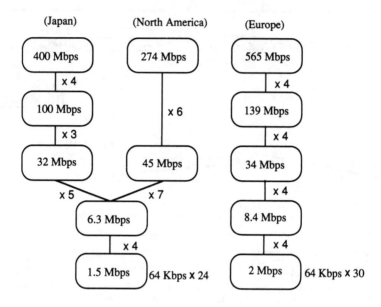

Figure 2.2(a) Digital hierarchy: conventional.

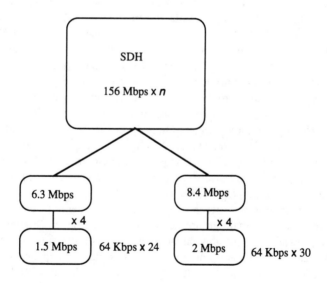

Figure 2.2(b) Digital hierarchy: SDH.

America and Japan, 2 Mbps in Europe) and group 2 (6.3 or 8.4 Mbps) of the earlier hierarchies.

NNI refers to the interface between nodes, which must perform a number of functions. As the primary interface of SDH, NNI was designed with the following goals in mind.

- It must be standard worldwide.
- It must be independent of network node functionality and of the signal type.
- It must be independent of the physical medium (e.g., coaxial cable, optical fiber, radio).
- It must be capable of forwarding control signals adequate to support the operation of an advanced network.
- It must be compatible with existing interfaces.
- It must be able to adapt to future service extensions and technology advances.

The NNI encompasses both 1.5-Mbps-class and 2-Mbps-class signals. The 9-row by 270-byte frame organization (illustrated at the top of Figure 2.3) was designed to satisfy this requirement.

In addition, it is important that the NNI be able to multiplex a wide variety of signal speeds without being conscious of the content or structure of the signals. The following multiplex units were established to support this goal.

- *Container (C).* A container wraps the digital signal to be multiplexed.
- *Virtual container (VC).* A virtual container is a container to which path overhead information has been added. Path overhead information, a part of the frame, contains information regarding the fundamental digital circuit (the "path"), and is used for network operation, supervision, and maintenance.
- *Tributary unit (TU)* and *administrative unit (AU).* A tributary unit is a virtual container to which a pointer has been added. The pointer indicates the starting position of the virtual container and obviates the need for phase matching of the virtual container to a particular frame location.
- *Synchronous transport module (STM).* The synchronous transport module is an administrative unit to which section overhead (SOH) has been added.

Figure 2.3 illustrates the organization of STM-1 and the functional relationships of overhead information and pointers. Figure 2.4 demonstrates the multiplexing stages from the 1.544-Mbps signal (the lowest level defined) to STM-1.

SDH establishes the foundation for a unified framework upon which services based on both 64-Kbps ISDN and 156-Mbps B-ISDN can be provided.

2.2.3 Looking from ISDN to B-ISDN

Figure 2.5 illustrates the general relationship between an ISDN or B-ISDN network and a user terminal. The user/network interface (UNI) is determined by the basic rate, as

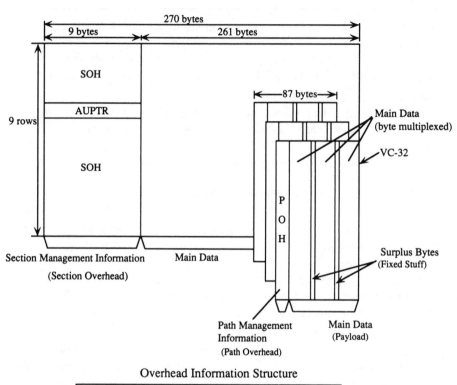

Overhead Information Structure

SOH	Frame synchronization Error checking Warning transmission Transport maintenance data link Transmission line switching control
AUPTR	VC-32 leading phase indication Frequency synchronization
POH	Error checking Warning transmission

Figure 2.3 The frame structure of the 156-Mbps synchronous interface.

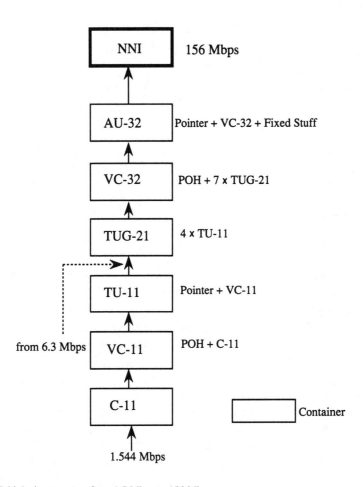

Figure 2.4 Multiplexing structure from 1.5 Mbps to 156 Mbps.

summarized in the table within the figure. The basic ISDN interface is defined as 2B + D, where B is 64 Kbps and D is 16 Kbps. The D channel is used for signaling or other packet communications services. The primary rate interface is standardized at nB + D, where n is 23 in North America and Japan and 30 in Europe, and the D channel is 64 Kbps. (ISDN service commenced at the end of the 1980s in some countries [4].)

B-ISDN is, of course, a network of the future, and as such, its design must take into consideration the services that will be offered in the future. While it is difficult to predict future services with confidence, it is thought that the primary services will be visual communication services: TV telephone, teleconferencing, video databases, high-speed data transfers (inter-LAN communications), high-resolution image transmission services, and integrated media services (broadcast and communications will be integrated). In contrast with existing networks, which are nearly entirely occupied by telephone

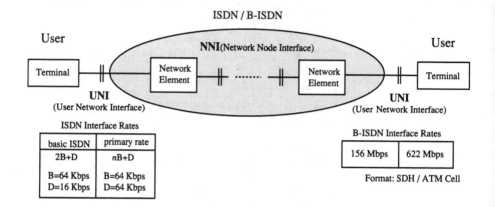

Figure 2.5 ISDN and B-ISDN network and user interfaces.

services, these future services exhibit an extremely wide range of bit rates and communications configurations. Therefore, future B-ISDN networks will have to possess the ability to

- Flexibly cover a wide range of rates;
- Handle a variety of traffic characteristics (both bursty and continuous traffic);
- Handle a variety of communications configurations (interactive and distributed, point to point, and complex).

It should be possible, by using an extended version of the narrowband ISDN UNI, to provide initial B-ISDN services to users from an SDH network as-is. However, with regard to the flexibility demanded by future ISDN services, the rigid SDH structure will likely prove to be problematic. The SDH rate hierarchy was originally determined based on the rates used for interexchange transmissions, and the higher rates are used only to multiplex a fixed number of lower rate circuits. This organization will be inefficient for providing a dynamically changing mix of services over a variety of fixed-rate channels, or for providing the bursty services under consideration as future B-ISDN services. These are the considerations that led to introduction of asynchronous transfer mode (ATM) for the B-ISDN interface. While the basic structure of the B-ISDN interface has been determined (e.g., two systems of 156 Mbps and 622 Mbps will be provided), the final details of the standard had not been fixed as of February 1992. However, what can be clearly stated is that in addition to SDH, the ATM concept will be included in these standards. We discuss the ATM concept in detail in the following section.

2.2.4 STM and ATM

Of the B-ISDN functions, those associated with switching and multiplexing are referred to as the *transfer mode*. CCITT Study Group XVIII selected ATM as the B-ISDN transfer mode. Contrary to what the name implies, ATM does not refer to asynchronous transmission at all. Rather, ATM is a method in which multiplexing and switching are performed in units of a particular type of packet, referred to as a *cell*. Something along the lines of "a periodic transfer mode" might have been more expressive of the actual behavior. In contrast with ATM, the earlier periodic multiplexing methods are referred to as synchronous transfer mode, or STM. Both STM and ATM can be thought of as rules for allocating the bandwidth required for a B-ISDN service. After due consideration of the wide variety of services and the demands that will be placed on B-ISDN systems, ATM has been chosen as the paradigm for the next generation.

ATM as a Protocol

In terms of the Open Systems Interconnection (OSI) model, B-ISDN network protocols can be seen as corresponding to layers 1 and 2 (the physical and data link layers), and part of layer 3 (the network layer). This relationship is shown in Figure 2.6. The layer constrained by the transmission-medium-dependent electrical and physical properties establishes bit-level timing, generation and reconstruction of the transmit frame (based on SDH), insertion of ATM cells into transmit frames, cell synchronization, and valid cell discrimination. These functions can be viewed as part of the physical layer. Furthermore, specifications related to cell multiplexing, demultiplexing, and switching can be viewed as the ATM layer. The adaptation layer is a further layer above the ATM layer that binds services to the ATM layer.

The Structure of ATM

ATM is essentially a scheme for wrapping information in a container called a cell. The cell is a container with a header and is the fundamental processing unit of ATM. The concept is very similar to traditional packet communications. The ATM concept differs from packet switching in that it predicates high-speed, low-error circuits (i.e., optical fiber technology). Thus ATM, as a transfer mode tuned for high-speed digital transmission, does away with the complex retransmission control that packet-switching protocols use to minimize a far higher error rate. Furthermore, while packet switching is mainly a switching technology, ATM subsumes both switching and transmission linkage.

The structure of the ATM cell is shown in Figure 2.7. The working cell size currently established by CCITT is 5 bytes of header and 48 bytes of data [7]. The header content differs for the NNI and the UNI. Users are concerned with the structure only of the UNI header, which is shown in Figure 2.7. The most important parts of the UNI header are the two label data fields, the virtual channel identifier (VCI) and the virtual path identifier (VPI). The label fields correspond to the time slot number used to discriminate channels and paths in STM. However, in STM, the time slot number is determined by the temporal position within the frame, so the channel and path are discriminated according to location. In contrast, ATM uses the label content as the basis for discrimination, making multiplexing

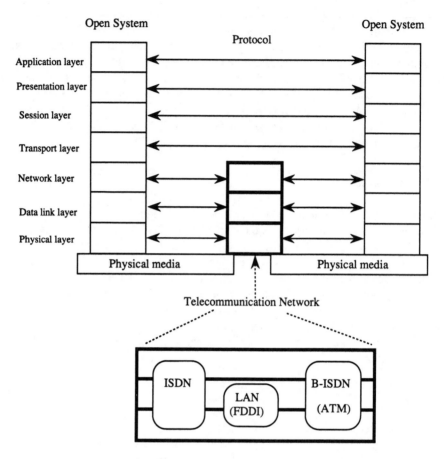

Figure 2.6 OSI reference model and B-ISDN.

extremely flexible and efficient. A virtual channel (VC) is established in response to a communications request (the traditional "call") from a terminal. A virtual path (VP) handles a group of VCs headed for a single target node. VPs can be semifixed or preassigned to handle situations in which a certain transmit capacity must be reserved between pairs of transmitting nodes for longer periods of time [8].

The Meaning of ATM for the User

If the functionality of ATM's VP and VC are used effectively, variable-rate circuits that respond to a variety of service requests can be provided. A simple comparison of the flexible circuit establishment functionality of ATM with that of the STM technique is shown in Figure 2.8. With STM, the channel speed allocated to a service is essentially

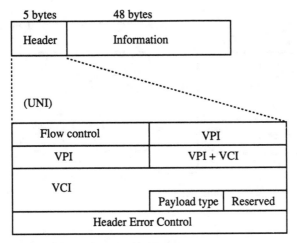

VCI: Virtual Channel Identifier
VPI: Virtual Path Identifier

Figure 2.7 ATM cell structure.

fixed, and the user is sometimes forced to employ extremely inefficient modes of circuit use. Since ATM recognizes channels by the cell label, it is possible to alter the channel capacity in response to service requests. Furthermore, this can be done over a high-speed circuit with 156-Mbps capacity. Accordingly, it is expected that the impact of ATM will be large for visual communication services that entail a wide range of bit rates. In the following chapters, we discuss in more concrete terms the impact on visual communication services.

2.3 VISUAL COMMUNICATIONS IN DIGITAL NETWORKS

In this section we discuss the characteristics of visual communication services based on digitalized visual media and their relationship with the digital network.

2.3.1 The Nature of Digital Images and Video

Digitized image signals are, in general, represented as two-dimensional planar digital signals called frames, and their characteristics within that two-dimensional space are determined by the number of pixels, the number of bits per pixel, and the form of each pixel's signal (the data structure in terms of the intensity and color). The higher the quality of an image, the more pixels (and bits) are required to represent it, and, accordingly, the higher the rate required to transmit the image.

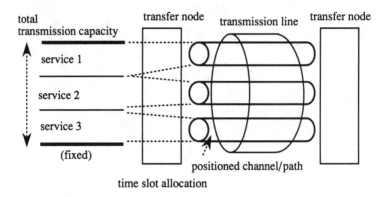

Figure 2.8(a) Variable-rate channels: path in STM.

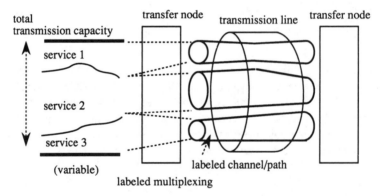

Figure 2.8(b) Variable-rate channels: path in ATM.

The characteristics of a visual communications channel can be specified by the signal transmission rate and the transmission delay time. The characteristics of digital image and video transmission services are shown organized by transmission rate (vertical axis) and transmission delay time (horizontal axis) in Figure 2.9. In this figure, a digital image service's access time is considered to be essentially equal to the transmission delay time (i.e., the time required for the signal to transit the network), and the transfer rate is calculated to transmit the signal within that time. In the following sections, we break out the digital image and video types shown in Figure 2.9 into two rough categories and examine each category in detail.

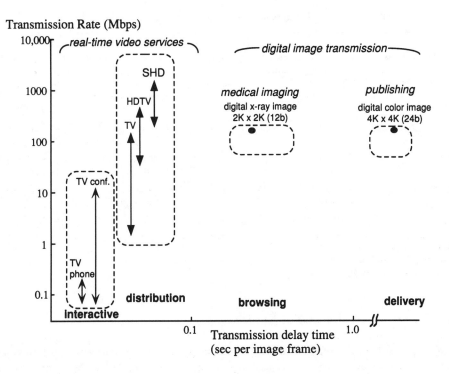

Figure 2.9 Digital images and video characterization.

Visual Communication Based on Real-Time Video

To provide a real-time video transmission service, the transmission delay time must be shorter than the small multiple of video frame period on average. Naturally, the same real-time nature is required for broadcasting normal television as well as HDTV. Although teleconferencing and TV telephone video are predicated on communication of video in real time, traditional TV telephone methods attempt to make do with very low transmission rates of 64 Kbps or a small multiple of 64 Kbps, lower than fundamentally required by these applications; these services adaptively lower the frame rate and thus transmit semimoving pictures. From the standpoint of communications form, teleconferencing and TV telephone are two-way and interactive, while broadcast video is unidirectional and distributive.

The basic resolutions and required transfer rates for the various types of digital video are summarized in Table 2.1.

Table 2.1

Information Volume and Required Transmission Rates for Various Image Types

Image Types	Spatial Resolution	Temporal Resolution	Color Representation	Bit Rate Required
Video telephony	176 × 144	30 fps	Luminance (Y), Chrominance (Cr, Cb)	64 Kbps × n $(n = 1,2)$
Video conferencing	352 × 288	30 fps	Luminance (Y), Chrominance (Cr, Cb)	64 Kbps × n
Digital TV	720 × 480 (NTSC) 720 × 576 (PAL)	30 fps	Luminance (Y), Chrominance (Cr, Cb)	30–45 Mbps or 140 Mbps
Digital HDTV	1920 × 1152 (European proposal)	30 fps	Luminance (Y), Chrominance (Cr, Cb)	30–140 Mbps
SHD Video	≥ 2048 × 2048	≥ 60 fps	R, G, B	≥ 150 Mbps

Notes: Y: luminance or brightness
Cr, Cb: color difference signals
SHD: super high definition

Visual Communication Based on Still Images

Applications that transmit still images include medical imaging, publishing, printing, and other image database search services. All of these applications can be categorized as distributive communications. The required transmission rates for these digital image transmission services depend on the image resolution and the required access time. In situations in which the user searches image data, referred to as browsing, the access time should not exceed one second. An access time of about one second is also desirable in medical imaging [9]. On the other hand, in applications such as publishing, all that is required is that the image actually be delivered, so there is no difficulty with transmission delays exceeding one second. In general, the faster the response required by the service, the higher the transfer rate must become. Strictly speaking, since the high rate is required only while the image is actually being transmitted, we are referring to the peak rate.

Figure 2.9 shows the transmission capacities required to assure an access time of one second for a sample medical image (2048 × 2048 pixels, 12 bit/pixel gray-scale x-ray image) and for a sample printing application image (a 4096 × 4096 pixel color image). Tables 2.2 and 2.3 show, for general digital images, how the transmission delay time changes with transmission rate.

Required transmission rates for visual communications such as these, based on digital video and images, cover a broad range, from 64 Kbps to 150 Mbps, and the rate (particularly the peak rate) provided by the communications network is a major factor in determining service quality.

Table 2.2
Transmission Rate and Estimated Delay for a Digital Gray-Scale Image (12 Bit/Pixel)

Pixels	Rate = 64 Kbps	Rate = 1.5 Mbps	Rate = 155 Mbps
512 × 512	49 (sec)	2 (sec)	0.02 (sec)
1024 × 1024	196	8	0.08
2048 × 2048	784	33	0.32
4096 × 4096	3,136	132	1.3

Table 2.3
Transmission Rate and Estimated Delay for a Digital Color Image (24 Bit/Pixel)

Pixels	Rate = 64 Kbps	Rate = 1.5 Mbps	Rate = 155 Mbps
512 × 512	98 (sec)	4 (sec)	0.04 (sec)
1024 × 1024	392	16	0.16
2048 × 2048	1,564	66	0.64
4096 × 4096	6,272	264	2.6

2.3.2 Burstiness of Digital Image and Video Transmission

If we consider the temporal variations in the content to be transmitted, it is apparent that the amount of information is essentially variable. For example, in transmitting still digital images, although a transfer rate as high as possible is desirable during access, during periods of no access, the amount of information to be transmitted is essentially zero. Even when transmitting continuous video signals, if the encoding scheme removes redundancy, volume will change continuously according to the content of the video.

Not only video, but also voice and audio signals exhibit temporal variations in the information volume resulting from the encoding process, which maintains a fixed level of quality. That is, these are all variable-rate information sources. Research on the efficient transmission of variable-rate information sources has a venerable history in the field of digital communications [10–12]. Since the networks available at the time of these early investigations could not feasibly provide variable-rate circuits, these researchers simulated variable-rate transmission by transmitting multiple sources as a group. With the advent of serious investigation of the high-speed packet and ATM networks discussed in Section 2.2, research into variable-rate signal transmission techniques to make effective use of network flexibility has come into its own [13–16].

2.4 IMPACTS AND ISSUES OF PACKET VIDEO TRANSMISSION

As we have emphasized, future digital networks, such as ATM, will provide an extremely high degree of flexibility in circuit data rates. At the same time, transmission rates for digital image and video are extremely varied, and are fundamentally time varying. Taking these two items into consideration, it is clear that packet video transmission is one approach to future visual communications. This section considers the impact of packet video and new technological issues. For the purpose of this discussion, we will assume high-speed packet transmission, such as is provided by ATM.

2.4.1 New Service Features

In principle, service features can be improved by increasing system flexibility. For example, in still digital image transmission, if the circuit rate is increased only during times when accessed images are transmitted, it would be possible to shorten the access time without degrading overall circuit utilization. For the transmission of digital video using sophisticated redundancy removal (compression) techniques, transient degradation can be avoided and fixed quality video transmission can be provided with variable-rate transmission. At the same time, it becomes easy to achieve multilevel quality video services with variable-rate transmission. We can also expect a statistical multiplexing gain by using variable-rate transmission and the resulting reduction in video transmission cost. Note, though, that while service features are improved, the user/network interface becomes more complex. New technological issues will be centered on maintaining the aforementioned merit of packet video transmission.

2.4.2 New Technological Issues

Video Signal Characteristics

In order to obtain statistical multiplexing gain by using variable-rate transmission of video signals, it is necessary to have a precise grasp of the statistical characteristics of packetized video signals. In conventional fixed-rate transmission, only the peak rate was required for network design and service provisioning.

The initial form of almost all video signals is that of an analog signal. (One exception is computer animation, in which the signal is digital from the start.) When such a video signal is simply digitized in a straightforward manner, the resulting digital data has a fixed rate (the sampling frequency multiplied by the number of bits per sample). However, by taking advantage of correlations either within a single image or between images, it is possible to reduce substantially the amount of information required to encode the signal. Since the degree of compression possible depends on the signal correlations, for a fixed level of distortion, the quantity of information after compression will vary over time according to the content of the video signal. This phenomenon is generally called *rate variability*. Here, we define the information content of visual media to be the amount of digital information remaining when the redundancy in the video signal has been compressed without distortion. The information content of a visual media signal can be thought of as approximately equal to the output of a high-quality, high-efficiency encoder. The statistical characteristics of video signals can be obtained by observing the rate variability. In order to understand the exact characteristics of packetized video signals, we also have to know the behavior of video encoding for packet video. If the characteristics could be accurately modeled, it would be a great help in designing networks.

Video Encoding Schemes

Contemporary coder and decoders (codecs) designed for fixed-rate transmission contain a rate buffer to smooth the rate variations naturally occurring in the compressed signal. Its purpose is to maintain, as closely as possible, a fixed quality level at a fixed transmission rate. Transient quality degradations, which are unavoidable with fixed-rate transmission, are reduced to a certain extent by controlling the encoding within the range of information volume that can be handled by the rate buffer and by adjusting the bit distribution. However, it is not possible to avoid large degradations when video signals are transmitted at low rates to hold down circuit costs. Constraints on the delay time also impose a limit on the buffer size that can be used to prevent degradation. As a result, transmission of video signals with redundancy removal is actually implemented as a fixed-rate transmission system in which the quality changes depending on the signal. (See Figure 2.10(a).)

The situation changes completely when a variable-rate circuit is available. As long as the maximum rate of the circuit is larger than the maximum rate generated by the video encoding algorithm, no rate buffer is required. In addition, so long as the information volume generated by the video encoding meets the established parameters of the user/ network interface, there will be no need for encoder rate control. Under these conditions,

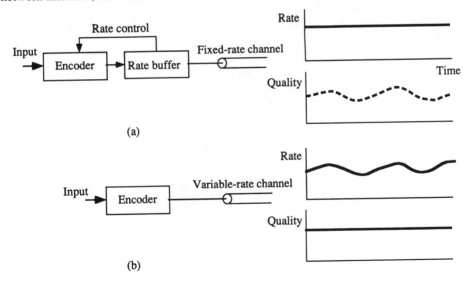

Figure 2.10 (a) Fixed-rate and (b) variable-rate (ideal case) transmission concepts.

video transmission based on ideal variable-rate encoding can be implemented, and video can be transmitted, at a fixed quality determined by the encoding algorithm. (See Figure 2.10(b).) (This situation can be viewed as equivalent to utilizing the network itself as a rate buffer of infinite size.)

Since a rate buffer and rate control are no longer necessary with ideal variable-rate encoding, the structure of the codec becomes extremely simple. Bit distribution in the encoding algorithm can consider only the need to maintain a fixed quality level. On the other hand, since the flexibility of the service is increased and the range of quality levels that can be selected is expanded, functions for controlling quality naturally become more complex. Furthermore, the ideal conditions described previously will not necessarily hold in actual variable-rate transmission; it is possible in practice for the peak rate generated by the video encoder to exceed the rate limit of the variable-rate circuit, or for the average rate generated by the encoder to exceed the average rate expected by the network. Accordingly, some form of rate control will probably be required even with variable-rate encoding.

User/Network Interface

Even though the provided communication channels for packet video are called variable-rate circuits or variable-rate channels, there is of course an upper limit to the bit rate, and the user must be aware of that limit in advance. At any rate, since the video signal peak rate can be predicted in advance from the characteristics of the video signal and the encoding algorithm, it will be possible to realize a state close to ideal variable-rate transmission for most of the transmission period by selecting an appropriate upper limit for the variable-rate circuit, and rate control should be required less frequently than with fixed-rate transmission.

From the standpoint of traffic management, the network administration would like to know the average load the user will apply to the variable-capacity circuit, since that has an impact on the network design. The network may impose rate control commands via the user/network interface, resulting in more complex control, considering the system as a whole.

Anyway, statistical characteristics related to network usage must be determined jointly by network users and administrators. There was no such need with earlier fixed-rate networks, and the network interface is thus more complex. The relationship of the user/network interface to network and service design is an important theme currently under discussion in ATM standardization [17–19]. (See Chapter 7.)

Delay-Time Jitter

Delay time in packet networks tends, in general, to be longer than in STM networks, due to the necessity of the packet assembly operation. However, for packet networks of the B-ISDN generation, because the packet size is small (53b for ATM networks) and transmission speeds are very high, the absolute increase in delay time will not be critical. In fact, for video transmission, the encoding processing delay will in general be larger than the delay due to packetization. In addition, because the codec's internal buffer can be decreased with the adoption of variable-rate encoding, the delay within the terminal will be shorter, so end-to-end delay time is not expected to be a problem. Studies indicate that in actual two-way real-time video transmission, an end-to-end delay of a few hundred milliseconds is acceptable, and ATM networks currently under consideration easily meet this requirement [20].

A new issue that must be addressed when using variable-rate circuits is delay-time jitter. Delay jitter arises from two factors: time-varying information is being converted into fixed-length packets, and contention or congestion can occur in the packet multiplexer and switching equipment. Variations in delay time due to packetization can be minimized relatively easily. For instance, when extremely low bit-rate signals are packetized, it suffices to generate dummy packets, which the receiver discards. (Of course, it is important not to generate so many dummy packets as to induce congestion.) The problem is variation in delay arising within the network. In fact, ATM network design consists in large part of estimating the variation in packet delay within the network, and thus has been the subject of intense investigation based on considerations of the traffic characteristics of various types of signals [21, 22]. Simply stated, the point of network design is to hold below a certain value the probability with which packet delay exceeds a certain maximum value, while minimizing the capacity of multiplexed circuit and that of network internal buffers. For the transmission of real-time signals such as video, delay times that exceed a certain level are equivalent to packet loss. Accordingly, correct estimation of network internal packet delay time distribution is critical for the variable-rate transmission of video signals.

Maintaining Timing Information

Delay jitter also gives rise to the problem of maintaining the transmission-side timing information (clock) [23]. In video transmission the frame frequency of the receiving terminal must match that of the transmitter. With these real-time services, frequency discrepancy leads to data overflow or underflow. Therefore, the receiver extracts a clock component from the data and matches the phase using a technique such as a phase-locked loop. In addition to delay jitter, in packet networks such as ATM, packet loss occurs with a given probability. As a result, maintenance of timing information requires techniques more complex than those used with STM networks.

Packet Loss Protection and Recovery

The influence of packet loss is not limited to the timing information maintenance problem, but also exerts a large influence on the image quality of the reproduced image or video. Of course, even in fixed-rate transmission, a variety of measures, such as refresh, are applied to handle the video quality degradation resulting from bit and other types of errors. Essentially similar techniques can be applied for video transmission over packet networks as well [24]. However, since loss of a packet results in the loss of more data at once than occurs with bit error, new techniques are required.

A rough classification of packet loss protection and recovery measures is shown in Figure 2.11. In this figure, measures are divided into three levels, starting with the signal source. Level 1 measures utilize characteristics of the signal, while Levels 2 and 3 measures differ based on the service type, and are independent of the signal. Level 2 measures are controlled by the user, while Level 3 measures are implemented within the network. These measures can be broadly separated into protection and recovery techniques but, as shown by the dotted lines in the figure, the various methods are interrelated and work together to fulfill the objective.

Level 1 measures are in essence techniques for preventing degradation from becoming conspicuous even when information is lost and are implemented in the signal processing algorithms. The *leaky coefficients* technique attempts to minimize the influence of information loss in algorithms that make use of signal correlations. The *layered coding* technique is used in combination with packet prioritization. These methods are discussed in detail in Chapter 6.

Level 2 techniques, executed by the user before the data is packetized, apply error prevention according to the importance of the data. Level 3 methods assume that packets are prioritized within the network and attempt to control the network so that the probability of packet loss is lower for more important data. While it is has not been definitively decided that networks will provide the types of control required by Level 3 functions, the concept of handling prioritized data within the network, that is, of providing service classes, is a generally adopted ATM network function [24]. Table 2.4 shows an example of service classes. Consider as an example the combination of layered coding and network internal priority as applied to variable-rate video signal transmission. Since video requires real-time transmission, it is handled as Class 1. The encoded data, having been classified by the layered coding algorithm, will be transmitted using high priority Class 1-a for the critical data, and Class 1-b for the remainder of the data. Section 7.2 discusses how to achieve the service classes with priority.

Recovery procedures consist of first identifying packet loss by some means and then performing some form of compensation. Perhaps the simplest compensation technique is the insertion of dummy packets at the receiving side. While signal-content-dependent postprocessing is effective for reducing quality degradation in voice signals, which exhibit strong periodicity, research to date [25] has shown that, with the exception of the simple *concealment* technique, which tends to hide the effect of errors, it is difficult to apply it directly to video signals. Techniques targeted at video signal compensation are discussed in Chapter 6.

2.5 SUMMARY

In this chapter we demonstrated how the match of flexible networks of the future, such as ATM, with the variable-rate characteristics inherent in digital image and video transmission

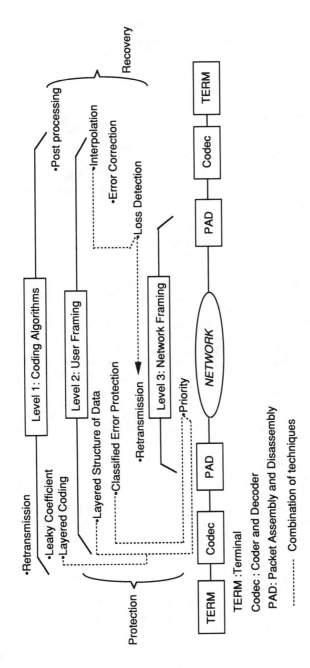

Figure 2.11 Packet loss protection and recovery.

Table 2.4
Example of Service Classes

Service Class	Quality	
	Delay	Loss
Class 1 (delay sensitive)		
Class 1-a	Better	Better
Class 1-b	Better	Worse
Class 2 (loss sensitive)	Worse	Better

signals creates the possibility of extremely efficient and attractive visual communication. We have also discussed the impact of such services and illuminated new technical issues that arise.

REFERENCES

[1] Recommendation G.711, "Pulse Code Modulation (PCM) of Voice Frequency," *CCITT Red Book*, Vol. 3, No. 3, 1985.

[2] Jayant, N. S., and Noll, P., *Digital Coding of Waveforms*, New Jersey: Prentice-Hall, Inc.

[3] *CCITT Blue Book*, Recommendations X.1-X.32, 1989.

[4] *IEEE Communications Magazine*, Special Issue on ISDN, Vol. 28, No. 4, 1990.

[5] Schoch, J. F., Dalad, Y. K., Redell, D. D., and Crane, R. C., "Evolution of the Ethernet Local Computer Network," *IEEE Computer*, Aug. 1982, pp. 10–26.

[6] *CCITT Blue Book*, Recommendations G.707, G.708, and G.709, 1989.

[7] Mintzer, S. E., "Broadband ISDN and Asynchronous Transfer Mode (ATM)," *IEEE Communications Magazine*, Sept. 1989, pp. 17–24.

[8] Sato, K., Ueda, H., and Yoshiyuki N., "The Roll of Virtual Path Crossconnection," *IEEE: The Magazine of Lightwave Telecommunication Systems*, Vol. 2, No. 3, Aug. 1991, pp. 44–54.

[9] Kohli, J., "Medical Imaging Applications of Emerging Broadband Networks," *Communications Magazine*, Vol. 27, No. 12, Dec. 1989, pp. 8–16.

[10] Haskel, B. G., "Buffer and Channel Sharing by Several Interframe Picturephone Coders," *Bell Syst. Tech. J.*, Vol. 51, Jan. 1972, pp. 261–289.

[11] Dubnowski, J. J., Crochiere, R. E, "Variable Rate Coding of Speech," *Bell Syst. Tech. J.*, March 1979, pp. 577–600.

[12] Koga, K., Iijima, Y., Kazumoto, I., and Ishiguro, T., "Statistical Performance Analysis of an Interframe Encoder for Broadcast Television Signals," *IEEE Trans. on Comm.*, Vol. COM-29, Dec. 1981, pp. 1868–1875.

[13] Verbiest, W., and Duponcheel, M., "Video Coding in an ATD Environment," *Proc. GSLB Seminar on Broadband Switching*, 1986, pp. 317–326.

[14] Ohta, N., "Variable Rate Video Transmission in Asynchronous Transform Mode Networks," presented at the *First International Workshop on Packet Video*, May 1987.

[15] Verbiest, W., Pinno, L., and Voeten, B., "The Impact of the ATM Concept on Video Coding," *IEEE Journal on Selected Areas in Communications*, Vol. 6, No. 9, Dec. 1988.

[16] Suzuki, J., Nakada, H., and Nomura, M., "Design Aspects of Variable Rate Speech, Audio and Video Coding for ATM Networks," *IEICE Technical Report*, CS88-56, pp. 25–30.

[17] Laser, A., Temple, A. and Gidron, R., "An Architecture for Integrated Networks that Guarantees Quality of Services," *Third International Workshop on Packet Video*, March 1990.

[18] Garrett, M. W., and Vetterli, M., "Congestion Control Strategies for Packet Video," *Fourth International Workshop on Packet Video*, Sept. 1991.

[19] Voeten, B., Van Der Putten, F., and Lamote, M., "Preventive Policing in Video CODECs For ATM Networks," *Fourth International Workshop on Packet Video*, Sept. 1991.

[20] Lee, S. H., and Wu, L. T., "Variable Rate Video Transport in Broadband Packet Networks," *Proc. SPIE Conf. on Visual Communications and Image Processing*, 1988, p. 955.

[21] Sato, Y., and Sato, K., "Virtual Path and Link Capacity Design for ATM Networks," *IEEE J. on Sel. Areas in Commun.*, Vol. 9, No. 1, Jan. 1991, pp. 104–111.

[22] Bae, J. J., and Suda, T., "Survey of Traffic Control Schemes and Protocols in ATM Networks," *Proc.. IEEE*, Vol. 79, No. 2, Feb. 1991, pp. 170–189.

[23] Singh, R. P., Lee, S. H., and Kim, C. K., "Jitter and Clock Recovery for Periodic Traffic in Broadband Packet Networks," *Proc. GLOBECOM '88*, Nov. 1988.

[24] Shimamura, K., Hayashi, Y., and Kishino F., "Variable-bit-rate Coding Capable of Compensating for Packet Loss," *Proc. SPIE Conf. on Visual Communications and Image Processing*, 1988, pp. 991–998.

[25] Suzuki, J., and Taka, M., "Missing Packet Recovering Techniques for Low-Bit-Rate Coded Speech," *Trans. IEICE, Japan*, Vol. J71-B, No. 12, 1988, pp. 1500–1510.

Chapter 3
Characterization of Video Sources

3.1 INTRODUCTION

As discussed in the previous chapter, a flexible communications network based on a technology such as ATM provides variable-rate high-speed channels, making variable-rate transmission possible even for real-time video signals. From the standpoint of network design, it is necessary to have a precise grasp of the statistical characteristics of these variable-rate signals. In particular, video signals, with their high-average bit rates, will have a large influence on network design. Moreover, since the signal rate variability characteristics depend strongly on the content of the video, we need to find approximating models that are better than a simple random generation model.

This chapter discusses the nature of video information sources and its impact on network design. First we discuss measures that quantify the rate variability characteristics of video signals (which we refer to here as the ''burstiness'' of the signal), taking the transmission of high-quality video over a B-ISDN network as a premise. We discuss the burstiness of video with quality levels corresponding to TV telephone, teleconferencing, and broadcast television, and present actual burstiness measurements (principally from our own research) of a variety of video signals. We attempt to determine useful guides for modeling video information sources using these results. However, since the nature of video information sources varies widely depending on the content of the video, the encoding scheme, and the quality required, caution is required in applying the results indicated here.

The discussions in this chapter assume that the reader has a basic understanding of video digital signal processing, encoding algorithms, and variable-length encoding. We recommend that readers lacking this background knowledge first read Section 5.4 or references [1,2].

3.2 FRAMEWORK FOR BURSTINESS EVALUATION

3.2.1 Video Sources

Our purpose in examining the temporal variability of video signals is to procure a guide to be used in designing the capacity of a digital communications network. Therefore, we focus on those types of video sources that are likely both to be transmitted over such a network and to exert an influence on network traffic volume. Given that the fundamental bit rate of current ISDN is 64 Kbps, and that of B-ISDN (broadband ISDN) is 156 Mbps, we are led to consider high-quality TV telephone, video conferencing (at least 64 Kbps per channel, any number of channels up to 1.5 Mbps), CATV, and broadcast television (10–150 Mbps) signals.

In particular, we do not consider extremely low bandwidth TV telephone or other services whose encoded rates are less than 64 Kbps. Designing the network to efficiently handle such low rate signals could easily result in increased network complexity and cost. Rather, we assume that high-quality image service is provided via B-ISDN, and consider services that distribute video with transmission quality equal to or better than that of teleconferencing for business use or CATV for general use.

Even when the video signals to be considered are limited in this manner, there is still a wide variation in the volume of information generated when encoding these signals, due to such factors as the content of the video or the type of encoding scheme used. Teleconference video images are nearly always images of people, usually viewed only from the waist up, and scene changes occur only rarely. With broadcast media, on the other hand, there are no limitations on the content, and scene changes are frequent. Since these two video types can be seen as the two extremes of video signals, we can obtain some degree of generality by analyzing each of them.

3.2.2 Encoding Schemes and Distortion

In Chapter 2 we defined the information content of a video signal as the data rate of the output of an encoder that removes redundancy. In practice, it is difficult to remove all redundancy, and the compression ratio achieved varies with the encoding algorithm. Furthermore, it is not possible to completely avoid distortion in actual encoding, and the amount of distortion will also depend on the video content. Therefore, changes in the data rate of the output of an actual encoding operation are not guaranteed to faithfully reflect changes in the information content of the original video signal. To obtain data that can be used to evaluate the intrinsic burstiness of video signals, a variable-rate encoding scheme must be employed that adequately removes redundancy while maintaining distortion at a constant level.

Distortion produced by video encoders can be classified as spatial (occurring within a frame), or temporal (occurring across frames), and it is not clear how these should be dealt with. For instance, 64-Kbps encoding schemes generally manipulate the frame rate, resulting in deteriorated temporal resolution (a form of temporal distortion), while encoding schemes used for television broadcast signals are dominated by spatial distortion. Evaluating both temporal and spatial distortion in an integrated fashion and maintaining total distortion at a fixed level is not practical.

In this chapter, we consider only intraframe (spatial) distortion as we evaluate burstiness. Although we ignore low bit rate encodings, such as TV telephone at extremely low bit rates, the results of our evaluations are applicable to television broadcast signals and adequate for our purpose, which is to obtain basic figures to use as guidelines.

Distortion Measures

From the point of view of a video service provider, one of the benefits of variable-rate transmission is that the image quality can be freely adjusted by adjusting the rate. Therefore, it is useful to identify some measure of burstiness such that, given an average rate, a fixed quality level (according to the chosen measure) could be maintained. Unfortunately, not only is it difficult (as discussed previously) to deal with many different varieties of distortion in a unified fashion, but also the perception of distortion is extremely subjective and difficult to quantify.

It is well known that quality (i.e., subjective quality) is not necessarily directly related to video signal distortion caused by encoding. In addition, technological arguments can be inappropriate in situations where the individual viewer's taste comes into play. In particular, the relationship between spatial and temporal distortion is subtle, and the problem of determining objective criteria that closely approximate subjective evaluations will remain an issue for the foreseeable future.

However, we are forced to select some practical solution. Since the measure to be held at a fixed level must be one that is easy to calculate, either the common signal to noise ratio (S/N ratio), or the weighted S/N ratio, which is the S/N ratio weighted by visual frequency characteristics, is used.

3.2.3 Time Scale for Burstiness Evaluation

Let us reconsider the definition of bit rate. Bit rate is the amount of information per unit time and is normally expressed in units of *bits per second*. Under the assumption that the rate is fixed, it does not matter if the time units are seconds or minutes. However, if the rate is variable, we must consider the time scale over which the bit rate is determined.

The factors that change the actual rate arise both from changes in the video signal itself and from the structure of the encoding algorithm. Video characteristics that give rise to rate changes can be categorized into locality within a single image (a video frame), signal correlation between frames, and the actual content of the video (e.g., cuts, scene changes). The time scale of variability differs for each of these phenomena. For instance, variation due to intraframe bias occurs within the cycle of a single video frame (1/30 sec in the NTSC standard), and variation due to a cut is on the order of a few seconds. The rate variation behavior will also change depending on the data buffering used by the encoding scheme. For example, the rate variation arising from bias in the signal within a frame will be seen externally as rate variation only if the encoding scheme adopted does not buffer frames. However, in current sophisticated encoding schemes, compression processing, such as transform coding, takes place after one frame of signal is stored in a small buffer (usually called a prebuffer). Therefore, since at least one frame's worth of data is output as a unit, the variation within a frame is, in practice, smoothed by the buffer.

An appropriate time scale over which to evaluate burstiness must take into account these kinds of variability factors. In this chapter, we assume an encoding scheme that has a buffer for one frame of data, and thus do not consider intraframe variations. Using the rate per individual video frame as a unit, we consider the variations within a single cut or scene. In order to consider variation across multiple cuts or scenes, we evaluate signals lasting from several minutes to several hours.

In Chapter 7, this problem is discussed, from the viewpoint of traffic management, as intervals of bit-rate monitoring.

3.2.4 Burstiness Measures

Some of the earliest work on information burstiness was by Kulzer et al., who defined burstiness simply as the ratio between the peak and average rates of the information [3]. In that work the average rate of audio information was found to be between 4 and 64 Kbps, with a burstiness level around 2 or 3. The average rate of conference video was hypothesized to be 1 Mbps with a burstiness of between 1 and 5, while standard video signals were seen as having an average rate of over 10 Mbps with a burstiness of between 1 and 2. However, measuring burstiness simply as the ratio of the peak and average rates is inadequate for the design of a communications network premised on statistical multiplexing of variable-rate information sources. In particular, when the types of service hypothesized here are first introduced, the number of sources being multiplexed on the network will not be adequate to validate the law of large numbers, especially for video sources, which are both high rate and very bursty.

Taking these issues into account, it is clear that there is a need to determine new measures for burstiness. The following list summarize some desirable qualities for new measures.

- The measures should not yield just statistical values, but values that capture the characteristics of the rate variation over time.
- The measures must be capable of evaluating the statistical multiplexing effect.
- The measures should allow easy modeling of video information sources.

Next, we describe several measures that have been investigated as fulfilling these kinds of conditions.

Bit-Rate Distribution

The most basic measures for characterizing bit-rate variations are measures that characterize the statistical distribution. Measures that have been used traditionally include the peak to average ratio (PAR) and the standard deviation to average ratio (SAR). Although these are simple and easily understood methods for roughly expressing the degree of burstiness, they cannot express the nature of the temporal variations. Of course, along with the average bit rate and the variance, they are quite adequate for approximating the required circuit capacity.

Autocorrelation Function

The autocorrelation function is a convenient basic measure for expressing the nature of temporal variations. If the volume of data in frame m is expressed as $x(m)$, then the autocorrelation $R(n)$ separated by n frames is defined as

$$R(n) = E[\{x(m) - M\}\{x(m + n) - M\}/\text{Var}[x(m)]] \tag{3.1}$$

Here, $E[\ ]$ expresses the expected value, and $\text{Var}[\ ]$ the variance, while M is the average bit rate ($E[x(m)]$).

Coefficient of Variation

Although the autocorrelation function expresses the temporal behavior of a discrete time series, it is not appropriate for expressing such phenomena as the signal delays that arise when a signal is buffered. We use the coefficient of variation as a measure to investigate the multiplexing characteristics when variable-rate signals are statistically multiplexed. The coefficient of variation is defined as follows for the total volume of information when an $n + 1$ sequence of data items is buffered.

$$C(n) = \{(n + 1)\ \text{Var}[x_b(n, m)]\}^{\frac{1}{2}}/E[x_b(n, m)] \tag{3.2a}$$

where

$$x_b(n, m) = \sum_{k=m}^{n+m} x(k) \tag{3.2b}$$

For an uncorrelated time series, the coefficient of variation $C(n)$ has a fixed value, while for a time series with a positive correlation, $C(n)$ increases with n. With this measure we can directly approximate the multiplexing performance of an infinite-buffer, single server queue. (See Chapter 4, Section 4.3.4.)

Distribution of Scene Durations

A scene change produces a singularity in the temporal variation of a video signal. The bit rate, which changes smoothly within a single scene, changes discontinuously at a scene change, and variations that have no correlation with the previous scene continue thereafter. The scene-duration distribution is introduced as a measure for characterizing this kind of discontinuous and irregular variation due to scene changes. Although scene changes are rare in teleconferencing, general broadcast video includes many scene changes, and the scene-duration distribution becomes an important measure.

Table 3.1 provides an overview of these measures.

Other Measures

The average duration of peaks is a measure that can be used to estimate the probability of buffer overflow. This measure indicates the average length of time that the information

Table 3.1
Definition of Burstiness Measures

Measure Type	Definition
Distribution	Measures that evaluate the shape of the distribution and the probability density distribution of the encoded bit rate evaluated in single frame units. Average bit rate. Standard deviation to average ration (SAR). Peak to average ratio (PAR).
Autocorrelation	$$R(n) = \frac{E[(x(m) - M)\,(x(m + n) - M)]}{\mathrm{Var}[x(m)]}$$ $x(n)$: the bit rate evaluated at frame n. $E[\ ]$: expected value, Var $[\ ]$: variance, $M = E[x(m)]$
Coefficient of variation	$$C(n) = \frac{\sqrt{(n + 1)\,\mathrm{Var}[x_b(n, m)]}}{E[x_b(n, m)]}$$ $x_b(n, m) = \sum_{k=m}^{m+n} x(k)$; a buffered sequence
Scene duration distribution	The probability density distribution of intervals between scene changes.

volume exceeds a given value. As it is implicit in the other measures already given, the average duration of peaks is not generally used as the principal measure of information content.

The moving average, a type of low-pass filter, can be applied to obtain bit-rate variability on a longer time scale from measures of the short-term variability. The width of the moving average's window is set according to the time scale to be studied. Equivalently, the moving average can be thought of as smoothing with a buffer of size equal to the width of the window.

In order to describe the tail of the bit-rate distribution, Garrett recently proposed using Pareto distribution along with Gamma [4]. This means that, in addition to mean and variance, the exponent giving the hyperbolic rate of decay of the tail can be used as a measure.

Garrett also used long-range dependence (LRD) to describe very high-order correlation caused by events that last a long time in the video process. Reference [4] is recommended to interested readers.

3.3 CHARACTERISTICS OF TELECONFERENCING VIDEO

Teleconferencing video consists almost entirely of scenes in which one or more people are facing the camera directly and talking. Scene changes occur only rarely. In this section we introduce samples typical of this kind of video and measure the bit rate of changes that occur in response to the motion of the characters.

3.3.1 Sample Video Sequences

We used two approximately 20-sec video sequences in which the speakers were imaged from the waist up while talking. Sequence (a) is a video in which the motion of the speakers is relatively large, and (b) is a video with little motion. A 256×240 pixel, 15-fps color video signal was used. Only the Y signal was used for the bit-rate measurements.

3.3.2 Encoding Schemes

Measurements were performed for three types of encoding schemes to investigate the differences in burstiness produced by differing encoding schemes [5]. Interframe differential PCM (DPCM) was used in scheme A, motion compensation plus interframe DPCM was used in scheme B, and motion transformation plus discrete cosine transformation was used in scheme C. These schemes were chosen because they are representative, and exhibit differing levels of effectiveness in removing redundancy. (Variable-rate encoding schemes are discussed in detail in Chapter 5.) Redundancy in video signals can be removed in the temporal and in the spatial domain. All the schemes selected here use interframe difference for the temporal domain; schemes B and C also make use of motion compensation. Scheme C uses discrete cosine transform (DCT) for the spatial domain. Subband coding is another method that can be used for removing redundancy in the spatial domain [6]. A little reflection, on the amount of information contained in a single frame, however, should convince the reader that bit-rate variability in video signals largely arises from redundancy in the temporal domain. That being the case, there should be little difference in the variability measured using DCT or subband coding.

Scheme A is the simplest algorithm, and its compression ratio is low. Scheme C is the most complex and so yields a high compression ratio. However, in principle, each of these algorithms uses interframe correlations, and the information volume changes with the motion of the imaged objects. Therefore, the burstiness characteristics should not differ greatly between these schemes. Table 3.2 gives an overview of these encoding schemes, and Figure 3.1 presents block diagrams. These encoding schemes were controlled so that the S/N ratio was maintained at a fixed value (around 43 dB).

3.3.3 Intrascene Bit-Rate Variations

Figure 3.2 shows the bit rate time variations when MC plus DPCM encoding is used. In this figure, the volume of data per frame (bits per frame) has been converted to the volume of data per second (bits per second). As can be seen from this figure, the bit rate changes smoothly with correlations depending on the motion of the subject. The impulse variations that can be seen in this figure are due to instantaneous image motions resulting from occasional camera jiggles while filming the scene.

Table 3.2
Comparison of Encoding Schemes

Encoding Scheme	Redundancy Removal Method	Variable-Rate Encoding Method
Scheme A: Interframe DPCM	Minimizes the variance due to interframe differences. Only sections with a large difference are quantized	Variable-length coding. (Huffman plus run-length coding.)
Scheme B: Motion compensation and interframe DPCM	The motion from the previous frame is predicted and only sections with a large remaining difference from the predicted signal are quantized	Variable-length coding. (Huffman plus run-length coding.)
Scheme C: Motion compensation and discrete cosine transform	The motion from the previous frame is predicted and only those sections with a large remaining difference from the predicted signal are further compressed to remove spatial redundancy using DCT	Variable-length coding. (Huffman plus run-length coding.) However, only the meaningful low-frequency components are quantized by using the DCT coefficient zigzag scan

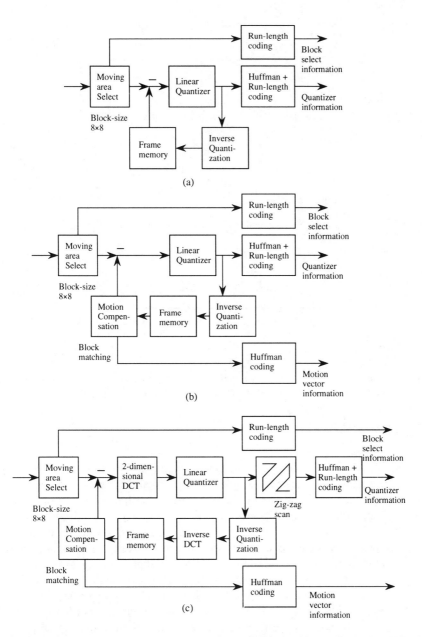

Figure 3.1 Encoding-algorithm block diagrams: (a) interframe DPCM, (b) MC + DPCM, and (c) MC + DCT.

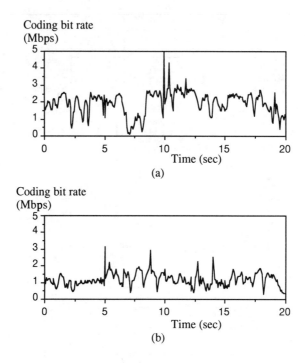

Figure 3.2 Bit-rate variation for video encoder output for (a) a video sequence with large movement and (b) a video sequence with small movement. (Algorithm: MC + DPCM.)

3.3.4 Bit-Rate Distribution

Figure 3.3 shows the distribution of bit-rate variation for each of the three types of encoding algorithm. These are bell-shaped, nearly normal distributions. However, in (a) the bit-rate distribution is shifted slightly to the high side. It can be seen that the shape of the distribution does not change significantly with the encoding algorithm used.

Table 3.3 shows the average value, ratio of standard deviation to average value, and ratio of peak to average value for these distributions. Here, all encoding algorithms were controlled to produce a per-frame video SNR of approximately 43 dB. Obviously, differences between average bit rates indicate the differing extents to which each algorithm succeeds in removing redundancy. (Note that the bit rates in Figure 3.3 have been normalized.) According to this data, the SAR for these distributions is about 0.3, and the PAR about 2 or 3. There is not a large difference in standard deviation between these algorithms. However, there is a difference in the maximum value; maximum values generated by the interframe DPCM algorithm are large and those generated by the MC plus DCT algorithm are comparatively smaller. The reason for this is that small motions of the subject are sensitively reflected as large increases in the bit rate by the interframe DPCM algorithm,

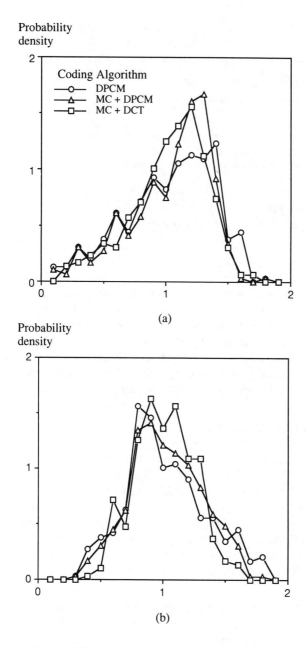

Figure 3.3 Distribution of encoded bit rate for (a) a video sequence with large movement and (b) a video sequence with small movement. The average bit rate is normalized to 1.0.

Table 3.3
Burstiness Results

Algorithm	DPCM		MC + DPCM		MC + DCT	
Video sequence	1	2	1	2	1	2
Average (bps)	2.7M	1.7M	2.0M	1.2M	252K	139K
SAR	0.4	0.2	0.4	0.3	0.3	0.3
PAR	3.4	3.1	2.5	2.6	1.8	1.9

Note: SAR = standard deviation to average ratio.
PAR = Peak to average ratio.

but increases in the information volume due to subject motion are held to a low level by the motion compensation plus DCT algorithm.

3.3.5 Autocorrelation Functions

Figure 3.4 shows the autocorrelation functions. In these graphs, the video frame interval has been converted to seconds. (The frame interval was 1/15 sec.) These graphs show that the autocorrelation decreases monotonically and exponentially for the first 0.5 sec, but that the correlations increase slightly again at 1 sec. This is probably because face and body motion has a natural period of about 1 sec during conversation. However, the autocorrelation is basically close to an exponential function. Furthermore, the differences in the shape of the autocorrelation between the algorithms are small.

3.3.6 Coefficients of Variation

Figure 3.5 shows the measured coefficients of variation. At $n = 0$, the coefficient of variation is about 0.3, but increases from 0.3 to 0.8 as n increases due to the positive correlations of the bit rate variation. Coefficients of variation will be used in Chapter 4, when we discuss multiplexing characteristics in the context of modeling.

Thus, in video images of people conversing, such as a single scene from a teleconferencing video, we find that the bit rate possesses an autocorrelation close to an exponential function, varies smoothly with the motion of the subject, and has an essentially normal distribution. Similar results are reported in [7–10].

3.4 CHARACTERISTICS OF BROADCAST TV

3.4.1 Sample Video Sequences

Broadcast television, unlike teleconference video, does not restrict its attention to scenes of people talking. Rather, minimal interscene correlations and frequent scene changes are

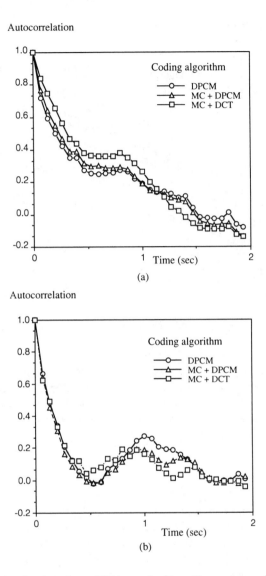

Figure 3.4 Autocorrelation function of encoded bit rate for (a) a video sequence with large movement and (b) a video sequence with small movement. Horizontal axis is normalized to seconds; 1 frame = 1/15 sec.

expected. In this section we use two video sequences of natural scenery that were shot on location (and taken from actual television broadcasts) as samples and present measurements of their burstiness. The main video data used are (a) a 10-min excerpt from "Shirarezaru Oze" ("Unknown Oze"), and (b) a 5-min excerpt from "Kita Arupusu

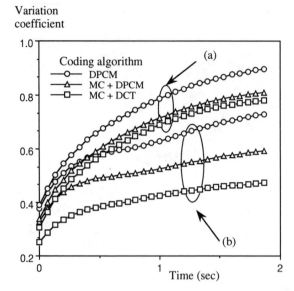

Figure 3.5 Coefficient of variation of encoded bit rate. Horizontal axis is normalized to seconds; 1 frame = 1/15 sec.

Natsu'' (''Summer in the Japan North Alps''). The video signal is a 512 × 480 pixel, 30-fps NTSC signal, with quality sufficient for use by a video distribution service. To get statistics on scene length, we also used two excerpts of television news programs and an excerpt from a movie, each about 13 min long. The original videos were color, but we used only the Y signal for these measurements.

3.4.2 Encoding Algorithms

This sort of video requires algorithms that produce higher quality output images than teleconferencing applications algorithms. In particular, cheating by reducing the number of frames and interpolating the motion is not acceptable. Given this assumption, we consider an adaptive intra/interframe encoding algorithm using the DCT to be the basic encoding algorithm. As we discussed earlier, insofar as bit-rate variability of video signals is generally dominated by temporal, rather than spatial, variability, it would make little difference were we to use other encoding schemes, such as subband coding.

Figure 3.6 shows the block diagram of this algorithm. First, the input signal is converted to the frequency domain in 8 × 8 pixel blocks using two-dimensional DCT. Next, interframe prediction is performed in the frequency domain. Different values are used for the prediction coefficients for each frequency component. The energy of the interframe difference signal is determined for each block; blocks for which the differential

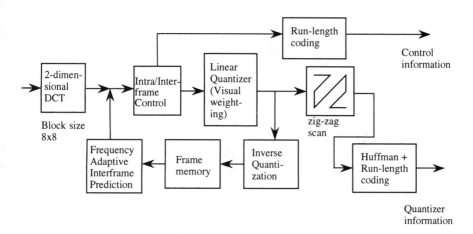

Figure 3.6 Adaptive intra/interframe DCT encoder.

energy is large are considered to be inappropriate for interframe prediction and encoding switches to intraframe prediction. The type of prediction used is transmitted as a separate control signal. By quantizing the signal with a weighting scheme that corresponds to human visual system frequency characteristics, it is possible with this algorithm to obtain an essentially fixed quality level with the quantization step held at a fixed width. The DCT portion of this algorithm essentially follows that of Chen [11].

3.4.3 Temporal Variations in Bit Rate

Figure 3.7 shows the results of investigating the bit rate time variations, including scene changes, for sequences (a) and (b). In order to simplify the processing in these computer-simulated measurements, the bit rate was evaluated in frame units, but evaluation was performed on only one frame every 5 sec within a given scene (when that scene was over 5 sec long), and the interval between the evaluations was interpolated linearly. Of course, several frames preceding and following each scene change were evaluated. Other than at scene changes, the bit rate was evaluated sparsely within long scenes. However, from the results of earlier investigations we expect that, compared to the size of variations due to scene changes, intrascene variations should show large correlations with smooth variation and that these approximations should be adequate for investigating the characteristics of long-term rate variations.

Although the intrascene changes are compressed in Figure 3.7, since the horizontal axis is in 1-min units, the bit rate exhibits radical step-functionlike changes due to scene changes. (If one views the actual videos, it becomes apparent that scene changes correspond almost exactly to the pulse-shaped inflection points.) On the other hand, there are a few places within scenes where the bit rate changes radically, for example, as a step function. Figure 3.8 shows an example of the rate variation around a scene change. The first half

Bit rate (Mbps)

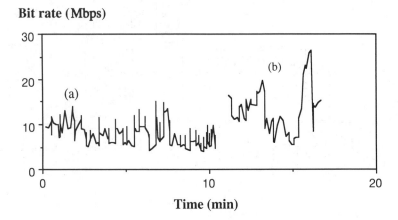

Time (min)

Figure 3.7 Bit-rate variation examples from two broadcast television programs: (a) "Unknown Oze," and (b) "Summer in the Japan North Alps."

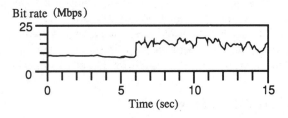

Figure 3.8 Bit-rate variation at a scene change in "Summer in the Japan North Alps."

is a scene taken with a fixed camera, and has little motion, whereas the second half was taken with a hand-held camera, and has large motion. This figure exhibits clearly the type of change in bit rate that occurs around a scene change.

This type of sharp change in bit rate is to be expected because the correlation with the previous frame is lost at the point of a scene change. Traditional encoding schemes, on encountering this sort of input, were forced to drop the frame rate in order to smooth out the peak in information volume. If the frame rate is fixed, the appearance of a frame that is uncorrelated with preceding frames causes the content of nearly every pixel in the image to change, and a traditional encoder is forced up to its maximum output bit rate. Of course, the frame immediately following a scene change may just happen to be correlated with the preceding frame, in which case such a peak in the bit rate will not occur. Models for peaks are discussed briefly in Chapter 4.

Measurement of the interframe bit-rate correlation within a scene shows a high correlation, similar to that observed in teleconferencing. For instance, Figure 3.9 illustrates the measured auto-correlation of the last half of "Summer in the Japan North Alps."

Autocorrelation

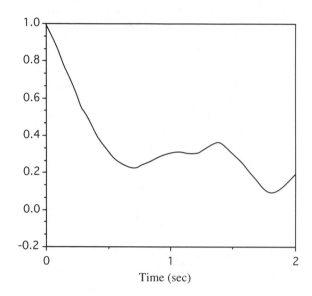

Figure 3.9 Autocorrelation function within one scene of "Summer in the Japan North Alps."

3.4.4 Bit-Rate Distribution

Figure 3.10 shows the bit-rate distribution for a combined video sequence of (a) and (b). (Data volume per frame has been converted to bits per second.) From this figure it can be seen that the rate distribution is skewed toward the low side. This is because most of the long sequences consist of images from within the same scene, and the redundancy has been removed successfully, resulting in a low rate, while sections involving scene changes or large motions occur only a small part of the total time. Similar characteristics are reported in [12].

For these video samples, the SAR is about 0.4 and the PAR is about 2.7, values not significantly different from those for the teleconferencing video samples. Generally, of course, these ratios vary from sequence to sequence. However, for long sequences, which include many differing scene types, the ratio probably settles down within some range. Data for longer video sequences are presented in Section 3.6.

3.4.5 Scene Duration

Since scene changes cause a discontinuous change in the bit rate, the statistical characteristics of scene changes are important for general video programming, which includes scene changes. The scene-duration distribution is a useful statistic. Figure 3.11 shows the results

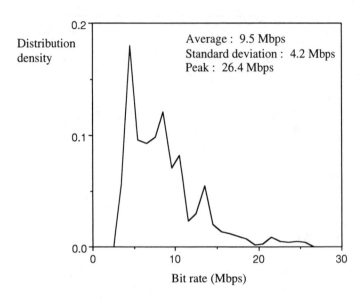

Figure 3.10 Bit-rate distribution example.

of investigating this distribution for the five video samples. This result shows that the form of the scene-duration distribution is essentially an exponential decay, but that extremely short scenes (of less than 1 sec) are rare. The average length of a scene is, from the range of data measured here, on the order of a few seconds. Figure 3.12 shows how the scene-duration distribution changes with the type of video. Figure 3.12(a) plots the natural scenery videos, "Unknown Oze" and "Summer in the Japan North Alps"; graph (b) plots a TV news program; graph and (c) plots a scene from the movie *Jaws* in which the camera work was particularly frenzied. The parameters of the approximately exponential distribution differ depending on the video content. The dotted line in Figure 3.12 is an approximation and can be viewed as an exponential distribution from which the short-scene portions have been removed. In Section 3.6.3 we present scene analyses of "VCR-quality" video.

3.5 OTHER REPORTED WORK

The idea of transmitting multiple multiplexed video signals efficiently by focusing on the variable-rate characteristics of the video signals existed long before high-speed packet-switching networks and ATM networks were investigated. Haskel carried out basic investigations into the characteristics of the TV telephone (they used the term "Picturephone") based on these ideas [13] and Koga et al. investigated multiplexed transmission of TV video signals [14]. Full-scale investigation of ATM networks began with [15,16], and experiments were performed by Verbiest et al. (cf. [12]). There are many other examples

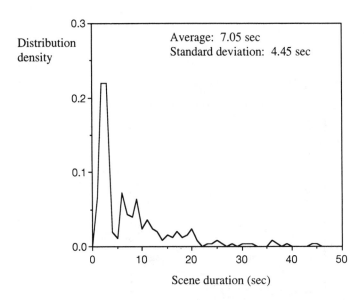

Figure 3.11 Scene duration distribution example. (Data from five video programs.)

of simulation and experimental investigations, and we recommend the references cited at the end of this chapter [17–20].

3.5.1 Characteristics of TV Telephone Video

At the time Haskel's research was performed [13], simple interframe differential encoding was used for Picturephone encoding to reduce the bit rate: only pixels with a large interframe difference were encoded and transmitted. This encoding is obviously variable rate, and a buffer was used for smoothing. If a buffer is inserted in each channel, and complete smoothing attempted, a large buffer size is required, and the transmission delay time will increase greatly. To avoid that delay, a high-speed line capable of handling the peak rate could be allocated to each channel, but that would result in an idle signal being transmitted on the channels during most of the time. The idea of multiple Picturephone encoders sharing a single high-speed circuit was investigated as a solution to this problem.

Figure 3.13 shows the basic form of the channel and buffer sharing system that was considered for this solution. Ultimately, data are transmitted over a single circuit using a large buffer. A switch is present ahead of the large buffer, and a label must be attached to the data specifying which source it came from. This is essentially the approach taken in contemporary ATM networks.

The video signals that Haskel worked with were 271-line 30-fps signals, where one frame consisted of 2 interlaced fields. The video signal was sampled at 2 MHz and

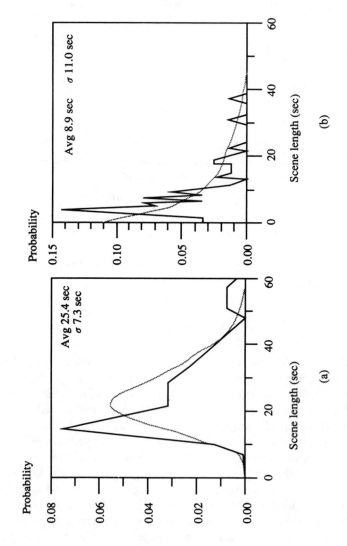

Figure 3.12(a,b) Scene-duration distribution examples: (a) "Unknown Oze" and "Summer in the Japan North Alps," (b) a TV news program.

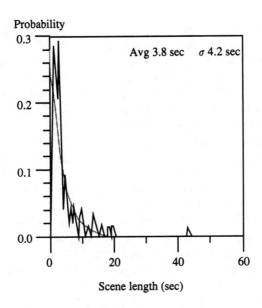

Figure 3.12(c) Scene-duration distribution examples: a scene from *Jaws*.

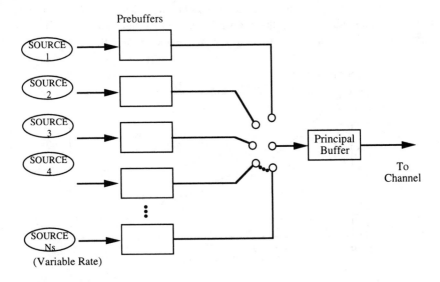

Figure 3.13 Overview of channel and buffer sharing system.

quantized at 8b. The content of the video used for evaluation was a sequence of about 1 hour of actual Picturephone conversation within a normal office.

The encoding scheme handled interframe differential values that exceeded a certain threshold as representing a significant change and encoded and transmitted those values. Haskel actually measured the probability with which the number of significant changes per video field exceeded a certain value. The number of significant changes can be thought of as being essentially proportional to the bit rate. The results of Haskel's measurements showed that when looking at a single video source, the probability with which the number of significant changes per video field exceeds a certain value is essentially an exponential. A similar result has also been shown for TV signals in [17]. Haskel then considered the size of the motion in the sample video, and classified video signals into 3 types: normal motion (category A), in which less than 11% of the pixels in a field change; active motion (category B), in which 11% to 25% of the pixels change; and violent motion (category C), in which more than 25% of the pixels change. For the 1 hour of sample video used by Haskel, 70% of the data fell into category A, 24% into category B, and 6% into category C. The standard deviation to average ratio (SAR) was approximately 1.0.

Since Picturephone videos consist of a single long scene, a high level of correlation can be expected. In fact, even for fields separated by an interval of one second, the correlation of the number of significant changes per field was measured at the rather large value of 0.5. Figure 3.14 shows the measured autocorrelation coefficient.

An important result of Haskel's work is the data concerning how long peaks in the information volume continue. He measured this as the *average duration of data peaks*, defined as follows.

If the number of significant changes per field exceeds threshold T at frame i and continues to do so until frame j, then the peak duration for threshold T is j minus i. The average value of this duration for a video sequence is the average duration of data peaks.

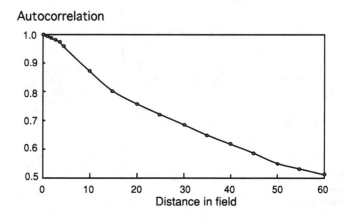

Figure 3.14 Normalized autocorrelation coefficient of the number of changes per field. (After [13].)

The following observations can be made from these measurements. Although the total period during which the information volume exceeds a threshold is short, whenever the information volume does reach a peak, that state will continue for at least several frames. Thus, when transmitting a single video source, this phenomenon can cause buffer overflow and result in a temporary degradation in quality. Haskel showed that it is possible to significantly shorten the average duration of data peaks by multiplexing transmission of multiple video sources. This phenomenon, illustrated in Figures 3.15 and 3.16, was suggestive of the quality improvements possible with variable-rate encoding, which is described in detail in Chapter 5.

The average duration of peaks has also been measured for the sample video data presented in the previous section [21]. Figure 3.17 shows the measured average duration of peaks for video sequences (a) and (b), as encoded with scheme C (motion compensation and discrete cosine transform). The results are similar to those reported by Haskel.

3.5.2 Measurement Results from Actual Video Encoders

Verbiest et al. used an experimental video codec system connected to an ATM network to carry out experiments on actual video data [10]. While all the work on characteristics described to this point involved only computer simulations, all of Verbiest's data are actual experimental values, and they handled enough data to investigate the statistical characteristics of even video length.

Three types of images were examined: (a) TV telephone (head and shoulder images called video telephony scenes), (b) teleconferencing (video conference scene: images of

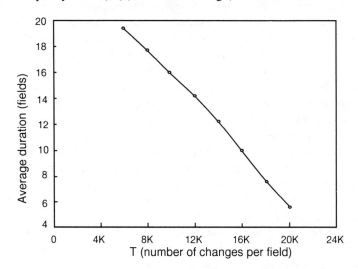

Figure 3.15 Average duration of peaks in the number of changes per field. (A peak starts when n rises above T and ends when n falls back below T.) (After [13].)

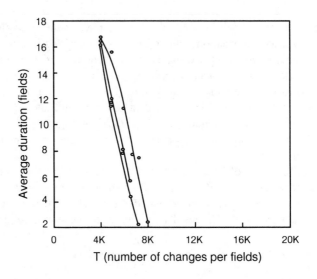

Figure 3.16 Average duration of peaks in the number of changes per field per source when data from five sources is combined. (After [13].)

two people seated at desks), and (c) broadcast television (sections of video actually broadcast from TV studios or over CATV).

A hybrid intra/interframe DPCM variable-length encoding scheme was used. The quantization step size and the conditional replenishment threshold value were selected based on the type of object video, and quality was adjusted so that quality degradation was not conspicuous. In particular, conditional replenishment was not used for studio TV scenes, since there were places where the image degradation was conspicuous. Figure 3.18 shows an overview of the experimental system.

Table 3.4 shows the statistical characteristics of the bit rate. The television scenes measured were on the order of several hours in length.

The autocorrelation functions for the three types of video were also measured (Figure 3.19). These measurements indicate that the characteristics of TV telephone and teleconferencing videos are almost identical. Both have large correlations between images separated by 2 or 3 frames, but have almost no correlation between images separated by 50 frames. In contrast, broadcast television video exhibits large correlations even between images relatively widely separated in time. For example, the correlation for images separated by 100 frames is approximately 0.5.

Let us compare these results with those we presented in Sections 3.4 and 3.5. As regards teleconferencing video, the correlation is slightly less, but nonetheless comparable, to the autocorrelation presented in Section 3.4. However, the correlation shown in Figure 3.19 for television video is larger than we obtained. A possible source of this difference

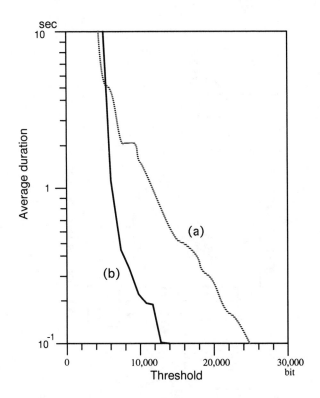

Figure 3.17 Example of average duration of peaks for (a) "Unknown Oze" and (b) "Summer in the Japan North Alps." (After [21].)

may lie in the fact that Verbiest used a simple DPCM encoding scheme, which has a low compression ratio.

Figure 3.20 shows Verbiest's measurement of average duration of peaks. This data shows that peak bit rates continue for long periods in broadcast television video. In particular, television video exhibits an interesting peak at a duration of approximately 1000 frames. The use of DPCM as an encoding scheme muddies the issue somewhat; but the data seem to imply that there is a tendency for action scenes to run for approximately 1000 frames.

Recently, Heeke [22–24] measured statistics of teleconference-type video signals coded with an H.261-based hardware video encoder. He demonstrated that rate distributions generated during time intervals within a very long video sequence varied considerably. Under the assumption that a coder can generate piecewise constant bit rates, and that the bit rate takes one of quantized rate classes, Heeke measured the holding and recurrence time for each quantized rate. His results show that the stochastic process of transitions

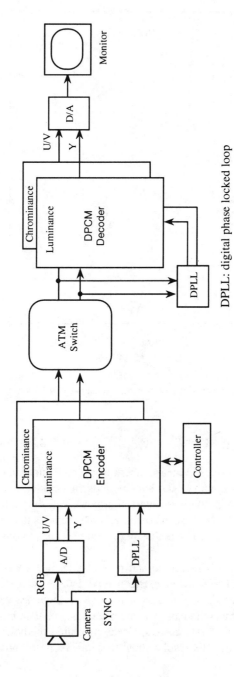

Figure 3.18 Experimental system based on variable-rate hybrid DPCM. (After [10].)

DPLL: digital phase locked loop

Table 3.4
Bit Rate Statistics for Four Video Types [10]

Video Type	Length	Average (Mbps)	Standard Deviation (Mbps)	Peak (Mbps)	SAR	PAR
TV telephone	30 min	4.3	2.9	19.1	0.67	4.4
Teleconference	30 min	4.9	2.3	15.1	0.47	3.1
Broadcast television						
Studio	12 hr	26.5	3.4	51.5	0.13	1.9
CATV	3 hr	16.8	4.3	44.7	0.26	2.7

Note: SAR = standard deviation to average ratio. PAR = peak to average ratio.

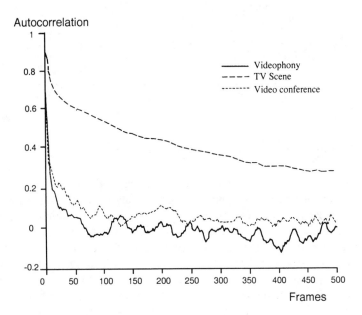

Figure 3.19 Comparison of autocorrelation function for three types of video signals [10].

between the quantized rates can be described by a Markov chain; the holding times of the rates follow a geometric distribution.

3.5.3 Scene Analysis of VCR-Quality Video

Judice et al. [25] analyzed actual entertainment videos, assuming a service that would distribute VCR-quality video over a digital packet network. Ten commercial videos were

Average peak length (frame)

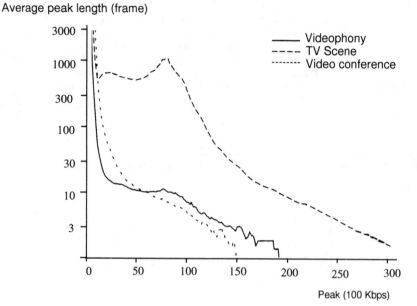

Figure 3.20 Comparison of average peak length as a function of peak height [10].

used as samples. These videos were divided into six categories depending on the amount of motion and type of camera work (they refer to this analysis as a *reduced video grammar*), and the scene lengths and bit rates were investigated. An actual multirate codec was used for the bit-rate measurements. The codec bit rate was set to achieve a fixed quality level for each of the above categories, and an average bit rate was computed by totaling the rates for one video. To hold the quality at a fixed level, two quality levels were set: a level at which degradation in quality relative to a VCR was clear and a level equivalent to that of the VCR. Although temporal variations in the bit rate were not investigated, the scene characteristics and statistical nature of many videos were investigated, thus providing important data.

The six types of scene category used are summarized in Table 3.5. The speed of subject motion was categorized as low motion, medium motion, high motion, or still. Camera motion was categorized as panning or zoom/roll-in. This table shows the results of analyzing a long (over 2-hour) movie (*The Shining*) for the length, number of scenes, and total number of bits for each of these categories. As this data shows, low motion scenes are unexpectedly common, and an average bit rate of about 1 Mbps is apparently adequate for VCR-quality transmission. Since the time for the still scenes was not provided, the average bit rate would be even lower if that data were included.

Table 3.6 shows the results of the analysis of 10 entertainment videos according to this scene categorization. Similar results can be expected for other films. The average scene length was about 7 sec, a value that agrees with the results of the previous section.

Table 3.5
Detailed Statistical Characterization of *The Shining* [25]

Grammar	Frames	Scenes	Seconds	Low Quality (Mb)	VCR+ Quality (Mb)
Low motion	142,980	214	4,766	2,441	4,883
Medium motion	15,990	134	533	541	811
High motion	750	8	25	38	76
Stills	666	666	N/A	115	173
Pans	22,590	91	753	288	768
Zooms/roll-ins	77,430	219	2,581	1,320	2,641
Total	259,740	666	8,658	4,743	9,351
Average bit rate				548 Kbps	1.08 Mbps

Table 3.6
Statistical Characterization of 10 Entertainment Videos [25]

Video Name	Average Bit Rate (Kbps) Low Quality	Low Motion (%)	Medium Motion (%)	High Motion (%)	Pan (%)	Zoom/ Roll-In (%)	Avg. Scene (sec)	Avg. Bit Rate (Mbps) VCR + Quality
The Shining	548	55	6	0.3	8.7	30	13	1.080
My Man Godfrey*	549	77	6	0	7	10	10	1.078
Eyewitness News†	543	87	2	0	3	8	6	1.070
Guiding Light†	571	69	8	0	12	11	4	1.114
Jeopardy†	576	94	2	1	1	2	4	1.124
Split Second†	570	80	5	1	2	12	6	1.107
Jane Fonda's Workout*	570	59	7	2	5	27	14	1.109
Donald Duck Movie*	606	66	14	0.3	14	5.7	5	1.154
Witness*	558	79	5	0.1	4.5	11.4	7	1.087
Temple of Doom*	613	59	10	0.3	10	20.7	3	1.166
Average	570	73	6	0.5	6.5	14	7.2	1.109

Note: * Three 5-min segments, randomly selected.
† One 5-min segment, randomly selected.

3.5.4 Scene-Independent Statistical Analysis of Long Video Sequences

Garrett [26,4] measured and analyzed the characteristics of very long video sequences with DCT-based coding schemes. Garrett's result represents a realistic full-length sample of entertainment video with a wide mixture of material using the movie *Star Wars* as the source. Garrett considered the stochastic bandwidth process of an intraframe coder as the number of bytes produced in each video frame. He found empirically that the marginal (or stationary) distribution of bytes per frame is not Poisson or Gaussian, but has a very slowly decaying tail. This distribution is well modeled by a Gamma body with a Pareto tail. His observation also presents that the video process contains events that last a long time and significantly correlate the bandwidth process for the duration of each event. This characteristic was measured using long-range dependence (LRD) [4].

3.6 SUMMARY

In this chapter, we investigated the variability, or burstiness, of a variety of video signals (particularly, teleconferencing video and broadcast television), as encoded by representative encoding schemes. In the process we employed a number of measures of burstiness that might be useful for modeling bit-rate variability. Of course, the results presented here are obviously not intended to address all possible types of video source, but they do provide us with a useful, basic handle on the characteristics of typical video sources. Using these results as a foundation, Chapter 4 attempts to build models of video sources.

REFERENCES

[1] Rao, K. R., Ypi, P., *Discrete Cosine Transform*, San Diego, CA: Academic Press, Inc., 1990.

[2] Woods, J. W. (editor), *Subband Image Coding*, Norwell, MA: Kluwer Academic Publishers, 1991.

[3] Kulzer, J. J., Montgomery, W. A., "Statistical Switching Architectures For Future Services," *Proc. ISS '84*, May 1984, 43-A.

[4] Garrett, M., "Contributions Toward Real-Time Services on Packet Switched Networks," Ph.D. Dissertation, Columbia University, 1993, Chapter 4.

[5] Nomura, M., Fujii, T., and Ohta, N., "Basic Characteristics of Variable-Rate Video Coding in ATM Environment," *IEEE Journal on Selected Area in Communications*, Vol. 7, No. 5, June 1989, pp. 752–760.

[6] Karlsson, G., and Vetterli, M., "Subband Coding of Video Signals for Packet Switching Networks," *Proc. SPIE Conf. Visual Comm. Image Processing*, Oct. 1987.

[7] Maglaris, B., Anastassiou, D., Sen, P., Karlsson, G., and Robbins, J., "Performance Analysis of Statistical Multiplexing for Packet Video Sources," *Proc. IEEE GLOBECOM '87*, Tokyo, Japan, Nov. 1987, pp. 1890–1899.

[8] Kishino, F., Ohta, N., Yasuda, Y., and Yasuda, H., "Packet Video Transmission Through ATM Networks," *Proc. GLOBECOM '89*, 1990.

[9] Shiino, H., Abe, M., Noguchi, O., and Shoji, Y., "Analysis of Multiplexing Characteristics of Variable Bit Rate Video Signals," *Third International Workshop on Packet Video*, March 1990.

[10] Verbiest, W., Pinno, L., "A Variable-Rate Video Codec for Asynchronous Transfer Mode Networks," *IEEE Journal on Selected Areas in Communications*, Vol. 7, No. 5, June 1989, pp. 761–770.

[11] Chen, W. H., and Pratt, W. K., "Scene Adaptive Coder," *IEEE Trans. on Comm.*, Vol. COM-32, 1984, pp. 225–232.

[12] Verbiest, W., Pinno, L., and Voeten, B., "The Impact of the ATM Concept on Video Coding," *IEEE Journal on Selected Areas in Communications*, Vol. 6, No. 9, Dec. 1988, pp. 1623–1632.

[13] Haskel, B. G., "Buffer and Channel Sharing by Several Interframe Picturephone Coders," *Bell Syst. Tech. J.*, Vol. 51, Jan. 1972, pp. 261–289.

[14] Koga, K., Iijima, Y., Kazumoto, I., and Ishiguro, T., "Statistical Performance Analysis of an Interframe Encoder for Broadcast Television Signals," *IEEE Trans. on Comm.*, Vol. COM-29, Dec. 1981, pp. 1868–1875.

[15] Cochennec, J. Y., Adam, P., and Houdin, T., "Asynchronous Time-Division Networks: Terminal Synchronization for Video and Sound Signals," *Proc. IEEE GLOBECOM '85*, pp. 791–794.

[16] Fujii, T., Nomura, M., and Ohta, N., "Characterization of Variable-Rate Interframe Video Coding for ATM-Based Networks," *Proc. GLOBECOM '88*, Dec. 1988, pp. 1063–1067.

[17] Seyler, A. J., "Probability Distribution of TV Frame Differences," *Proc. IREE*, Australia, 1965, p. 355.

[18] Maglaris, B., Anastassiou, D., Sen, P., Karlsson, G., and Robbins, J. D., "Performance Models of Statistical Multiplexing in Packet Video Communications," *IEEE Trans. on Comm.*, Vol. 36, No. 7, July 1988, pp. 834–844.

[19] "Packet Speech and Video," *IEEE Journal on Selected Areas in Communications*, Vol. 7, 1989.

[20] Huang, S. S., "Source Modeling for Packet Video," *Proc. ICC '88*, 38.7, June 1988.

[21] Nomura, M., Fujii, T., and Ohta, N., "Bursty Information Characteristics and Modeling of a Variable-Rate Video Coding," *Transaction of IEICE (Institute of Electronics, Information and Communication Engineers)*, Japan, Vol. J71-A, No. 2, Feb. 1988, p. 432 (in Japanese).

[22] Heeke, H., "Realtime Measurements on Output Signals of VBR Video Codecs," *Fourth Int. Workshop on Packet Video*, F3, August 1991, Kyoto, Japan.

[23] Heeke, H., "Statistical Multiplexing Gain for Variable Bit Rate Video Codecs in ATM Networks," *Int. Journal of Digital and Analog Comm. Systems*, Vol. 4, 1991, pp. 261–268.

[24] Heeke, H., "A Traffic Control Algorithm for ATM Networks," *IEEE Trans. on Circuits and Systems for Video Technology*, Vol. 3, No. 3, June 1993.

[25] Judice, C. N., and Jaquez, M. J., "High Compression Coding of Entertainment Video For Packet Networks," *IEEE COMSOC International Workshop on Future Prospects of Burst/Packetized Multimedia Communications*, Osaka, Japan, Nov. 1987, pp. 4–5.

[26] Garrett, M. W., Vetterli, M., "Congestion Control Strategies for Packet Video," *Fourth International Workshop on Packet Video*, Kyoto, Japan, Aug. 1991.

Chapter 4
Video Signal Modeling for Prediction
of Statistical Multiplexing

4.1 INTRODUCTION

Information source modeling is extremely important for high-speed packet switching and ATM network design. Since the channel capacity for each information source is allocated dynamically in these networks, source models are especially important for estimating required channel capacity. Analyses based on the queuing theory under the assumption of random packet arrival were effective for earlier packet networks carrying data generated by computers and data processing terminals. However, since there are strong correlations within audio, image, and video signals, when a network must carry these signals the random arrival assumption may no longer be valid. Therefore, the information sources must be modeled in some fashion.

It is easy to understand how speech signals can be modeled via approximations to the human vocal tract, and significant results have been achieved in voice coding and synthesis by using linear models. The most distinctive feature of speech signals, from the standpoint of information volume variations, is that in conversational speech there are alternating periods of signal (speech) and no signal (silence). Thus research on speech-packet transmission is less concerned with the information volume variations within a signal period than with modeling the probability of switching between the signal and no signal states in the speech signal. Since the encoded bit rate for speech signals is at most 64 Kbps, it is acceptable to treat the maximum rate during intervals of speech as 64 Kbps. (If we accept slightly degraded speech quality, speech coding for telephone at 32 or 16 Kbps may be acceptable. In this case, we can treat the maximum rate during intervals of speech as 32 or 16 Kbps.) We can also approximate the rate during silent intervals as 0 Kbps. Therefore, in light of the fact that the smallest unit of bandwidth provided by a digital line is 64 Kbps, we can ignore the bit-rate variability (64 Kbps) within the speech periods and approximate the bit rate using the pattern of speech and silence interval durations. Queuing analysis for packetized speech has, in fact, traditionally been performed in this way [1].

However, video signal encoding can require as much as several megabits per second, far exceeding the 64-Kbps unit of bandwidth, and the range of bandwidths exhibited is very broad. Therefore, a simple model, such as the on/off model used for speech, is not very appropriate. Furthermore, in dealing with video signals, it is difficult to imagine how a generation model analogous to vocal tract models describing speech generation could be created. Instead, we must construct an empirical and approximating model based on the burstiness characteristics described in the previous chapter.

In this chapter, we will use the characterizations of video sources developed in Chapter 3 to build models of video signals. The purpose of these models is to allow us to reflect the properties of video signals in the design of communications and transmission networks. We will use the models we develop to infer the statistical multiplexing characteristics that can be expected in such networks. As we present each model, we will also strive to make clear which statistics the model is useful for evaluating and under what conditions the model can be expected to hold.

4.2 FUNDAMENTAL SUPPOSITIONS FOR VIDEO SIGNAL MODELING

4.2.1 Why Model Video Signals?

The most important aim in constructing models of the bit-rate variability of video signals is to create an aid for designing the future communications networks that will carry multiplexed video signals. More concretely, we want to predict

- The delay arising from statistical multiplexing;
- The buffer size required for multiplexing;
- The bandwidth required for carrying the multiplexed data.

The prediction of delay arising from statistical multiplexing is needed in order to tackle the problem of delay in video transmission services. The buffer size is useful for estimating the scale of multiplexing equipment. The required transmission bandwidth, in conjunction with traffic analyses of voice and data signals, is necessary to design the overall bandwidth of the communications network.

Predictions such as these can be performed using either simulations based on actual data or mathematical analysis. The difficulty of preparing and handling large amounts of data means that simulations with actual data are practical only on a small scale. On the other hand, if an appropriate model is used to generate data, very accurate predictions can be made. However, in regions of extremely low probability (e.g., estimation of maximum delay), the calculation becomes intractable. Therefore, we want to use analysis in these regions, but it is important to pay careful attention to the purpose for which the model was constructed and to its applicability in the region under study.

4.2.2 Classification of Bit-Rate Variability of Video Signals

Video signals exhibit several fundamental periodicities, the most basic being the frame period. Most current video encoding algorithms operate on the frame as a unit, and the correlations in the output bit rate naturally reflect the frame period. This is the *structural* periodicity of video signals; moving images are created by repeatedly displaying two-dimensional images at a fixed rate. As we saw in the previous chapter, the sources of bit-rate variability can be roughly classified as scene changes, motion within the scene, and changes in the fineness of two-dimensional detail in the video. Table 4.1 classifies these bit-rate variations into three classes based on their time scale.

Long-term variations arise mainly from content changes in the video due to scene changes. The bit rate changes as a step function, and the rate variability characteristics following the scene change are completely different from those preceding the scene change. This kind of variation occurs on a time scale of about a few seconds on average in broadcast television signals.

Short-term variations arise because of image content variations within a single scene, for example, from motion of the imaged objects. These bit-rate variations are temporally correlated and change smoothly. The time scale ranges from a few frames to a few seconds. As we saw in Figure 3.4(b) of the previous chapter, there are two types of temporal correlations: short-term correlations, which fall off exponentially, and long-term correlations, which persist over a time scale of about 1 sec.

In considering these short- and long-term correlations, we use the volume of information per processing unit of the encoding algorithm (usually one frame) as our unit of measure.

Table 4.1
Classification of Bit-Rate Variations

Type	Time Scale	Causes	Characteristics
Interframe variability			
Long-term variability (multiple scenes)	Several seconds or longer	Scene changes	Discontinuous variation, differing statistical characteristics before and after the change
Short-term variability (intrascene)	Between 1 frame period and several seconds	Subject motion, camera motion, pattern variations	Smooth variations with temporal correlations, with occasional large variations due to subject and camera motion
Intraframe variability	Less than 1 frame period	Spatial variations of the characteristics within an image	Variations that have a periodicity due to image scanning or block processing

Intraframe variations arise because of scanning lines or processing blocks within a single frame. As noted in the previous chapter, most interframe encoding schemes incorporate a buffer of a given size that absorbs these intraframe variations so that they do not appear externally as bit-rate variations. The need to consider intraframe variations could arise in situations where there is a requirement to minimize the size of the buffer used in the terminal. In this case, data would be directly output to the network without passing through a buffer. However, a buffer is an absolute necessity for the networks we are considering, in which the packet size is only a few tens of bytes and the video bit rate is at least 64 Kbps and usually on the order of several megabits per second. Thus there is no need to consider intraframe variations; in fact, most research in this area has taken the frame as the minimum unit of consideration.

Based on these considerations, a video information model can thus be divided into three layers. In actual modeling, determining which layer(s) to consider will depend on the encoding algorithm, the packetization scheme, the type of video being transmitted, and other factors. In this chapter we will suppose transmission over contemporary short-packet-length ATM networks and focus our discussion on models based on interframe variations.

4.2.3 Multiplexing Technique

Since the purpose of modeling is to evaluate statistical multiplexing of video signals and the delays to which it gives rise, we must hypothesize a system model as a basis for this evaluation. A simple multiplexing model, such as that shown in Figure 3.13 of the previous chapter, is generally used, and we shall assume that model in this discussion [2–4]. In the model, N independent variable-rate video sources are smoothed by individual prebuffers, multiplexed, and accumulated in the principal buffer. We assume that variations within single video frames are smoothed by the prebuffers. The output of the prebuffers is multiplexed in units of cells or fixed-length packets, each of which includes an identification of the source. The number of packets generated per unit time is proportional to the information rate of each video source. The packetizer is referred to as a packet assembler/ disassembler (PAD). Packets accumulate in the principal buffer and are output to the high-speed channel in first-in first-out (FIFO) order. Figure 4.1 illustrates this multiplexing model. The primary focus of our investigation of statistical multiplexing of video signals is to arrive at an estimate of the distribution of packet delay due to multiplexing [5]. On the basis of this estimate, for a given number of video signals (whose characteristics are known), we are able to estimate the transmission capacity that should be assigned, the resulting utilization, and the required buffer size. We are able to produce estimates for the probability of buffer overflow and the rate of packet discard.

From this point of view, we require that our model parameters be easily determinable from the characteristics of actual video information sources and that the model be amenable to simulation and analysis.

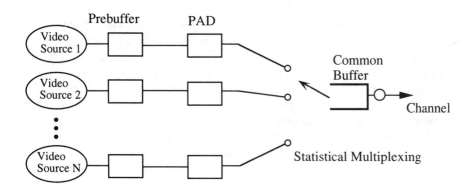

Figure 4.1 Statistical multiplexing model.

4.3 MODEL OF INTRASCENE VARIATION (SHORT-TERM VARIATIONS)

Models of bit-rate variation within a scene are useful in describing video sources with few scene changes, such as teleconferencing video. From the previous chapter's discussion of statistical characteristics of video signals, we know that teleconferencing video signals have a bell-shaped bit-rate distribution and high interframe autocorrelations, and that the form of the autocorrelations is essentially exponential. Based on these observations, in this section we present an autoregressive process model for simulation use and a model based on discrete-state Markov processes for analytical use. The section concludes with a discussion of a method, which uses coefficients of variation, that does not directly model bit-rate variations, but can be used for evaluating average delay times.

4.3.1 Autoregressive Process Model

We have shown that the temporal correlations of intraframe bit-rate variability tend to follow an exponentially decreasing curve [4]. This indicates that a model based on autoregressive (AR) processes is very natural. However, while an AR process model can be used relatively simply to simulate the characteristics of a single video information source, it is not particularly appropriate for evaluating statistical multiplexing. In this section, we investigate the closeness with which AR process models can express the bit-rate variability characteristics of video information sources and the extent to which AR process models can be used to evaluate statistical multiplexing characteristics.

In the following we use distributed average-value discrete-time AR processes as a model. The definition is

$$x(n) = X_M + y(n) \tag{4.1}$$

$$y(n) = \sum_{m=1}^{M} a(m)\, y(n-m) + be(n) \tag{4.2}$$

Here, $x(n)$ is the information volume (in bits) per frame for the nth frame, X_M is the average value of $x(n)$ (i.e., $E[x(n)]$), $e(n)$ is a normally distributed random number with average value 0 and variance 1, M is the degree of the model, and $a(m)$ is a parameter of the model. Strictly speaking, the model's statistics (average rate, variance, correlation, etc.) are made to match those of actual video signals by adjusting X_M, b, $a(m)$, and the degree of the model. Generally, the higher the degree of the model the better the approximation. Determining the most appropriate degree to use depends on the degree of precision desired in the final evaluation of statistical multiplexing.

For simplicity, the modeling example below uses a degree of 1.

A Sample Application of the AR Process Model

To model the video data shown in Figure 3.4 of Chapter 3, encoded with the MC + DCT algorithm, we proceed as follows. The correlation functions for scenes (a) and (b) are taken to be exponentials with the distance 1 correlations being 0.838 and 0.622, respectively. The value of $a(1)$ is made to correspond to the correlation at distance 1 (time unit). Because $e(n)$ in (4.2) is a normally distributed random variable with average value 0 and variance 1, we can choose a value for coefficient b that will cause the variance of the model to correspond to those of the video scene. For instance, with a first-order AR process model, the coefficient b and variance V are set as

$$V = b^2/[1 - a(1)^2] \qquad (4.3)$$

The parameters actually used for scenes (a) and (b) are summarized in Table 4.2.

Figures 4.2 and 4.3 compare the probability density distributions and autocorrelation functions of the AR processes derived in this manner with those of the actual video signals. It is apparent that the information distribution is approximated with an AR process that is close to a normal distribution. The short-term correlation (up to about 0.5 sec) is quite well approximated, but the order of the AR process model must be increased to approximate longer term correlations. Maglaris has also demonstrated that AR models provide an excellent approximation of the bit-rate variability of video information [2]. The adequacy of this model is determined by its usefulness for evaluating the statistical multiplexing effect.

Table 4.2
Parameters for AR Process Models

Sequence	$X_M(Kbps)$	$a(1)$	b	V
Scene (a)	252	0.84	0.163	0.09
Scene (b)	139	0.62	0.235	0.09

Probability
density

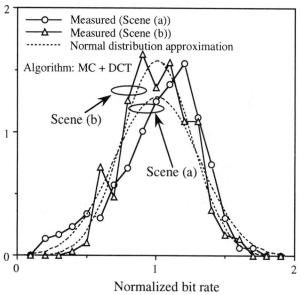

Figure 4.2 Probability density distributions for the AR process.

4.3.2 Evaluation of the Statistical Multiplexing Effect Using the AR Model

It is possible to infer statistical multiplexing characteristics, for conference video and the like, by modeling intrascene variation with AR models. In this chapter, we investigate the utility and practicality of this approach.

When N independent AR processes are multiplexed, the statistical characteristics of the resulting multiplexed signal can be derived from the characteristics of the individual AR processes.

If $y(n)$ represents the signal which results from multiplexing N AR processes $x_1(n)$, $x_2(n), \ldots, x_N(n)$, we have

$$y(n) = \sum_{i=0}^{N-1} x_i(n)$$

Here, if we assume that the $x_i(n)$ are mutually independent, the average and variance of $y(n)$ are simply the sums of the average and variance. In other words,

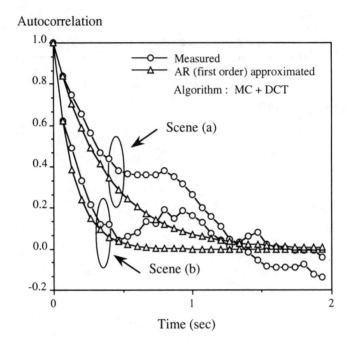

Figure 4.3 Autocorrelation functions for first-order AR processes.

$$E[y(n)] = \sum E[X_i(n)]$$

$$E[y(n)y(n + S)] = E\left[\sum X_i(n)\sum X_i(n + S)\right] = \sum E[X_i(n)X_i(n + S)]$$

$$(4.4)$$

These sums are to be calculated from $i = 1$ to N.

It follows, then, that if an identical AR process is used to model each video information source, the bit-rate variability of the multiplexed signal can also be approximated by an AR process whose parameters are identical to those of the original AR process and whose average and variance are simply multiplied by N. However, using AR processes, it is extremely difficult to obtain analytically the delay due to buffering. For that reason, we use a simulation to evaluate the delay due to buffering.

Simulation Methods

The multiplexing model of Figure 4.1 is assumed, that is, the output of the encoder is assumed to be smoothed by a prebuffer. The smoothed output of N video sources is packetized, and packets are added, one at a time, to a common buffer. The content of the buffer is read and transmitted at a constant rate.

If $X(n)$ is the volume of information entering the buffer in unit time, and C (a constant) is the volume of information leaving the buffer in unit time, then the volume of information accumulated in the buffer, $B(n)$, can be approximated as

$$B(n + 1) = \max[B(n) + X(n) - C, 0] \tag{4.5}$$

Note that we have assumed that the common buffer is always large enough, that is, it never overflows. As a result of this simplification, this model cannot accurately simulate situations in which overflow will occur. However, by using a large enough buffer, the probability of overflow can be reduced to arbitrarily small values. Thus, it is important to remember that this simulation is restricted to domains where the probability of buffer overflow is so small as to be negligible. Similarly, we will ignore the problem of underflow. Since underflow can be addressed by having the system generate dummy packets, this is not a difficulty for our simulation.

In order to evaluate the suitability of our AR models, we carried out simulations using three types of video source: an actual video signal, a random signal with no correlations, and a first-order AR process. These simulations are described below.

Simulation A: multiplexed video sources. Sequences of actual variable-rate video signals were artificially generated and multiplexed as follows. The sequence of bits per frame values produced by encoding scene (a) video data (from Chapter 3) by the MC + DCT algorithm was randomly shifted and the resulting streams multiplexed. Since the amount of data is small, the accuracy of the calculated delay-time distribution is poor for regions of low probability. However, statistical multiplexing characteristics close to actual values are obtained for regions of high probability.

Simulation B: random series (zero-order AR process). A random series model with no temporal or interseries correlations was used, and the average and variance of the distribution were matched to those of an actual information source (scene (a) encoded by the MC + DCT algorithm).

Simulation C: first-order AR process. This simulation used the first-order AR model described in the previous section.

Figure 4.4 plots simulated average delay times generated by multiplexing various numbers of sources. The horizontal axis is the number of video information sources multiplexed, and the vertical axis is the average delay time. The utilization parameter was varied between 0.8 and 0.9. (The utilization, sometimes referred to as traffic intensity, is defined as the ratio of the sum of the average bit rates to the total channel capacity.) As the plot illustrates, an evaluation based on random sequences underestimates the average delay time. The reason is apparently that, because we are multiplexing a series with no temporal correlations, less data accumulates in the buffer than would with a real video signal. The error becomes more significant as the utilization increases, because high

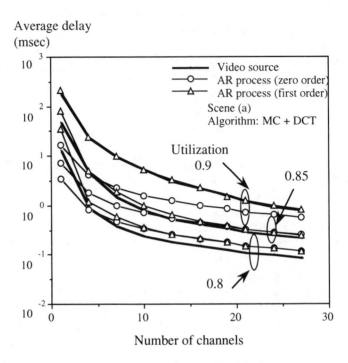

Figure 4.4 Average delay evaluation using the AR model.

utilization indicates that the average bit rate of the individual video sources is high, and the discrepancy in the estimated delay will therefore be large. In addition, if the number of multiplexed sources is small, the influence of the error introduced by the random series grows. These two tendencies are independent of the absolute value of the average bit rate; they depend only on the relative bit rate as compared to the channel capacity.

The simulation using a first-order AR process, which takes into account correlations, agrees well with the result of multiplexing actual video sources. One point in which the results differ (due to differences between actual information sources and assumptions in the model) appears in the lower right of the figure: the AR process model gives a longer delay time than occurs with actual information sources. This is due to the fact that the shape of the distribution for the actual information sources is not quite normal. Specifically, the probability distribution of the encoded form of actual video signals has values smaller than the normal distribution for regions of high information volume. Therefore, the simulation can be improved by limiting the generation of regions with a large information volume. Of course, Figure 4.4 also makes clear the effectiveness of statistical multiplexing: the average delay is smaller for larger numbers of multiplexed channels [4].

Figure 4.5 shows the delay-time distribution. It is clear that the distribution of delay predicted using AR processes is close to that observed when real video signals are

1 - Cummulative distribution

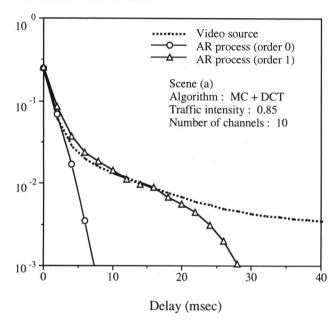

Figure 4.5 Delay distribution evaluation using the AR model.

multiplexed. However, using first-order AR processes, the delay is underestimated for long delay values (above 20 ms in this example). In general, large delay occurs with low probability, and in order to accurately evaluate this region, the size of the data set must be increased using a simulation based on models of higher order.

These results show that first-order AR processes can be used to model the bit-rate variations of video that does not include scene changes (the majority of teleconferencing video meets this definition), and that the multiplexing characteristics (the delay-time distribution) can be inferred. Let us, then, consider in what domain valid estimates will be obtained. Since the delay will in general be underestimated in regions of large delay, some caution is required. The range for which valid estimates can be obtained will vary with the average bit rate of the signal, the transmission circuit utilization ratio (if multiplexed transmission is used), and other factors. For example, with an average bit rate of 140 Kbps and a transmission circuit utilization ratio of 0.85, it is expected that first-order AR processes can provide correct estimates for delay times of up to 20 ms. Modeling that takes long-term correlations into account is possible if higher degree models are used.

Figure 4.6 shows an example of delay times evaluated using first-order AR models for various numbers of multiplexed channels. The model was evaluated for utilization parameter values ranging from 0.75 to 0.9. From these results, it can be expected that the

1 - Cumulative distribution

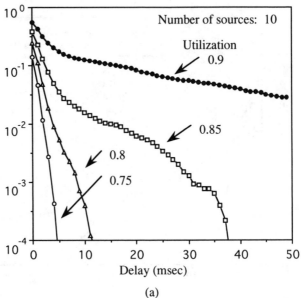

(a)

1 - Cumulative distribution

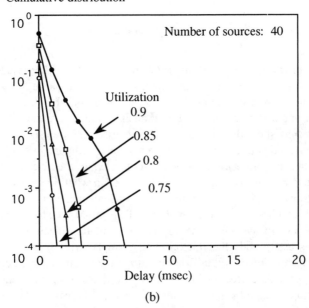

(b)

Figure 4.6 Examples of delay distribution evaluated by a first-order AR model for scene (a). Algorithm: MC + DCT; (a) number of sources: 10; (b) number of sources: 40.

average delay will be under 5 ms when 40 channels of teleconferencing video are multi-plexed at a utilization ratio of 0.85. Since the processing time per frame in a standard codec is about 15 ms, this is an acceptable value for transmission system delay time. (Of course, other aspects of the system, such as the delay time for the audio signal, must also be considered.)

The multiplexing results indicated earlier can be considered to be essentially established for the multiplexing of video signals whose bit-rate variations meet the first-order AR process assumptions, for example, teleconferencing video with an average bit rate on the order of 100 Kbps. However, it is necessary to remember that this simulation assumes no buffer overflow. That is, the fact that the buffer will overflow with nonzero probability at high utilization rates must be taken into account.

4.3.3 Markov Process Model

Although AR process models allow multiplexing characteristics to be easily simulated, logical analysis of AR processes is problematical. For example, in analyzing the network packet loss ratio, one wants to evaluate regions of extremely low probability density, preferably with an analytic technique.

Here, we introduce two estimation methods based on Markov models to evaluate the multiplexing effect using analytic methods.

1. *Discrete-time, discrete-space Markov model.* A discrete-time, discrete-space Markov model was proposed by Huang [6,7]. In this model, packets generated by video sources are multiplexed, with the number of multiplexed packets quantized into M levels. The model is represented by a finite-state machine, where each state corresponds to a possible packet-rate level (see Figure 4.7). Each state has three possible transitions: increase, decrease, and remain at the same level. The steady-state probability of being at each state can be calculated iteratively. It was shown that, with appropriate parameters, the model can describe the probabilistic behavior of the aggregate packet rate when video sources are statistically multiplexed.

2. *Continuous-time, discrete-state Markov model.* Maglaris et al. demonstrated a method based on a continuous-time, discrete-state Markov process that is also

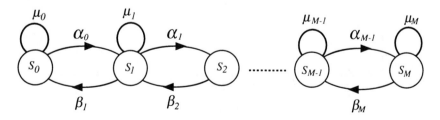

Figure 4.7 Discrete-state, discrete-time Markov model for aggregate packet rate. (After [7].)

effective for this type of evaluation [2]. This is a fluid approximation model and can be thought of as a model for draining water from an unlimited reservoir that is collecting water from a source; fixed-rate draining occurs, with on and off periods having an exponential distribution. However, bit rates take on only discrete quantized values and are assumed to be sampled at random Poisson times in the time domain. In other words, bit rates can be seen as switching between states with discrete values, and the time spent in each state is given by a random Poisson time sequence. Figure 4.8 shows an example of sampling the bit rate at Poisson times. The quality of the approximation can be improved by reducing the amount of information in a quantized step and increasing the sampling rate. Furthermore, instead of modeling the individual information sources, the total bit rate of N independent video information sources is modeled. These assumptions enable an analytic approach. Modeling is carried out by matching the information volume, the number of states, and the transition probabilities for each state in the model to the average rate of the sum, the variance, and the autocorrelation functions for N actual information sources.

To model the actual video sources, Maglaris et al. used the observation that, as intrascene bit-rate variations are smooth, their sum should exhibit no sudden jumps, to produce a Markov model like the one shown in Figure 4.9. This is a type of birth/death Markov model, and only transitions to adjacent states are generated. There are $M + 1$ states, and the state quantization step size is A bits per frame. States towards the left have low bit rates, and those to the right, high rates. The probability of a transition to a higher bit-rate state is higher for low bit-rate states and decreases as the bit rate increases. The

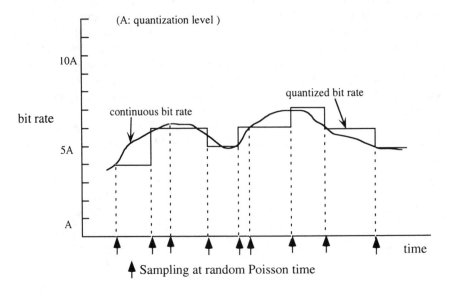

Figure 4.8 Poisson sampling and quantization of the source rate.

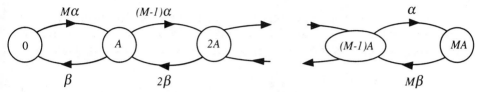

$$M\alpha \qquad (M-1)\alpha \qquad\qquad\qquad\qquad \alpha$$

$$\beta \qquad\qquad 2\beta \qquad\qquad\qquad\qquad M\beta$$

Figure 4.9 State-transition diagram for an aggregate source model.

probabilities change in the opposite direction for transitions that decrease the bit rate. The transition probabilities were given by Maglaris as

$$\left.\begin{array}{ll} r_{i,i+1} = (M-i)\alpha & i < M \\ r_{i,i-1} = i\beta & i > 0 \\ r_{i,i} = 0 \\ r_{i,j} = 0 & abs(i-j) > 1 \end{array}\right\} \qquad (4.6)$$

Here, $r_{i,j}$ is the probability of the transition from state i to state j, and α and β are parameters that determine the transition probabilities.

The earlier work that this model is based on includes an analysis of multiplexing characteristics based on the binomial model of Anick et al. and the application of that model to the analysis of statistical multiplexing in voice packet systems [8,9]. Daigle et al. used "minisources" whose on state represents an "active talkspurt" and whose off state represents a silence interval. Analysis proceeded by superposing these minisources. Minisources transit between the two states with probabilities α and β. The information source model produces zero information volume in the off state and the unit information volume (A) in the on state (see Figure 4.10). Figure 4.9 can be viewed as the superposition of M independent minisources with only one state transition at a time: state k is the state in which k minisources are in the on state, producing k units (i.e., kA) of information.

The model in Figure 4.9 is based on the assumption that the bit rate of multiplexed data for video without scene changes does not make large stepwise changes.

The steady state of the sum of minisources model of Figure 4.9 can be derived from queuing theory as described in [10, p. 107].

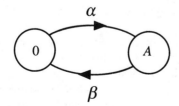

$$\alpha$$
$$\beta$$

Figure 4.10 Minisource model.

Taking the sum of the bit rates of N video information sources to be $X_N(t)$ and the number of quantized bit-rate steps (i.e., the number of states) to be M, the steady state probability that $X_N(t)$ is in state k is given by the following binomial distribution.

$$P\{X_N(t) = kA\} = \binom{M}{k} p^k (1-p)^{M-k} \qquad p = \alpha/(\alpha + \beta) \tag{4.7}$$

The average value $E[X_N]$, the variance $V_N(0)$, and the autocovariance $V_N(t)$ are derived from

$$E[X_N] = MAp \tag{4.8}$$

$$V_N(0) = MA^2 p(1-p) \tag{4.9}$$

$$V_N(\tau) = V_N(0) \exp[-(\alpha + \beta)\tau] \tag{4.10}$$

Modeling proceeds by fitting the parameters in (4.4) to (4.7) to the statistical values obtained from actual video data. That is, taking the average value, variance, and autocovariance of the information sources to be $E[X]$, $V(0)$, and $V(\tau) = V(0) \exp(-\alpha\tau)$, and assuming that the information sources are independent gives

$$E[X_N] = NE[x] \tag{4.11}$$

$$V_N(0) = NV(0) \tag{4.12}$$

$$V_N(\tau) = V_N(0) \exp(-\alpha\tau) \tag{4.13}$$

This allows the relationships between the statistical characteristics of the individual information sources and the parameters in Maglaris' model to be easily determined.

Analysis of Multiplexing Characteristics

Anick et al. derived analytically the steady state solution for the case where data generated from the type of information source described accumulates in a buffer and is read out at a fixed rate [8].

Let i minisources be in the on state at time t, and let the probability that the information accumulated in the buffer at that time does not exceed x be $P_i(t, x)$. Let S be the rate at which information is read from the buffer (i.e., the transmission rate). Anick's analysis gives the following result (we recommend the interested reader look up the details in the reference). Letting $F_i(x)$ represent the steady-state value of $P_i(t, x)$ the following differential equation is obtained.

$$(iA - S)dF_i(X)/dx = (M - i + 1)\alpha F_{i-1}(X)$$

$$+ (i + 1)\beta F_{i+1}(X) - [i\beta + (M - 1)\alpha]F_i(X) \qquad 0 < i < M \qquad (4.14)$$

This can be expressed as follows using vector $\mathbf{F}(x)$ to represent $(F_0(x), \ldots, F_M(x)^T$.

$$\left. \begin{array}{c} \mathbf{F}(X) = [F_0(X), \ldots, F_M(X)]^T \\ \\ \mathbf{D}d\mathbf{F}(X)/dt = \mathbf{R}\mathbf{F}(X) \end{array} \right\} \qquad (4.15)$$

Here $\mathbf{D}$ is a diagonal matrix whose elements are $(iA-S)$ and $\mathbf{R}$ is a transition matrix whose elements are the transition coefficients of (4.3). Assuming $iA \neq S$, the above equation can be solved using the eigenvalue and eigenvector of $\mathbf{D}^{-1}\mathbf{R}$. That is, the probability $F(x)$ that the information in the buffer is less than x is given by the sum of the solutions of $F_i(x)$ of the equation above. Since the probability that the information accumulated in the buffer exceeds x is $1-F(x)$, this function is useful in evaluating multiplexing characteristics. (The function $1-F(x)$ is called the survivor function.) In general, packets that do not fit into the buffer are discarded since they cannot be accumulated. Also, packets whose delay exceeds a particular value can generate a situation equivalent to packet loss even if they do arrive at the receiving end, because they cannot be decoded in time to meet the real-time conditions for video signal playback. Although this model cannot model the behavior under packet loss, it is possible to use the survivor function for estimating the probability of packet loss.

Number of Minisources Required

As mentioned earlier, it is necessary to increase the number of discrete states (i.e., the number of minisources) to a certain extent to acquire a good approximation. Maglaris et al. computed the survivor function $(1-F(x))$ for TV video signals (average bit rate 3.9 Mbps) using conditional replenishment, with the number of minisources as a parameter [2, p. 841]. Their result was that for a single video source, varying the number of minisources from 10 to 80 did not result in a large change in the analytically derived survivor function. Therefore, they argued that 10 was an adequate number of minisources. In particular, since varying the number of minisources from 20 to 80 results in almost no change, they concluded that in multiplexing N video sources, it will suffice to use 20 × N minisources.

What can we expect when teleconferencing video is encoded at low bit rates? We investigated multiplexing characteristics for various numbers of minisources, using as input data scene (a) from Chapter 3 encoded by the MC + DCT algorithm. Figure 4.11 shows analyses of delay time characteristics for various numbers of minisources based

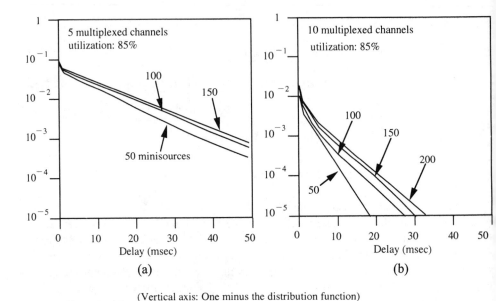

(Vertical axis: One minus the distribution function)

Figure 4.11 Delay distribution parameterized by number of minisources. (a) 5 multiplexed channels, utilization: 85%; (b) 10 multiplexed channels, utilization: 85%.

on the Markov model discussed previously. This result indicates that 100 minisources produces a reasonable estimate for multiplexing 5 sources, and 200 minisources suffice for 10 sources. This agrees with the results of Maglaris et al. (i.e., $N \times 20$).

Comparison of Delay Characteristics Computed by Various Models

Here, we compare results from the first-order AR model of the previous section with the analytic results from the Markov model, while considering the results from the simulated multiplexing of actual video signals. Figure 4.12 uses the data from Chapter 3's scene (a), encoded with the MC + DCT algorithm, as a model for a single video information source. Figure 4.12(a) shows the delay characteristics for 10 multiplexed channels as the utilization ratio is varied over the range from 80% to 90% and 4.12(b) shows the delay characteristics as the number of multiplexed channels is varied from 5 to 20, with the utilization ratio fixed at 85%. These results show that, in general, an AR process simulation underestimates the sections where the delay time is long for low utilization cases, as compared with analytic results based on a Markov model. Conversely, Markov model analyses underestimate the delay in sections where the delay is short (5 ms or shorter). This tendency also holds for other video signals. (See Figure 4.13.)

In order to determine how accurately these models can quantitatively estimate delay, experimental results of multiplexing a wider variety of video types will have to be

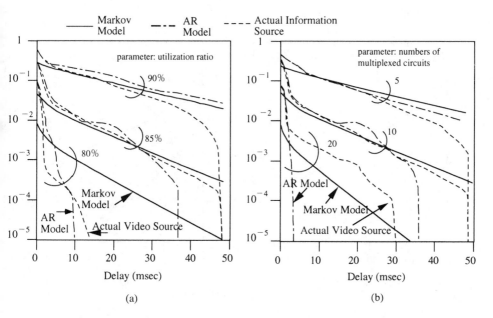

Figure 4.12 Comparison of delay characteristics for (a) ten multiplexed video sources at varying utilization ratios and (b) a fixed utilization ratio of 85% with varying numbers of multiplexed video sources. (Model based on the video signal characteristics of scene (a) encoded by the MC + DCT algorithm.)

compared. However, we can state that since these models do provide a rough estimate of multiplexing results, they can be a useful aid to system design.

4.3.4 Evaluation of Average Delay Time Using Coefficients of Variation

If there were no temporal correlations in variable-rate video signal sequences, the queuing theory, whose validity has already been established, could be used to analyze the characteristics of the statistical multiplexing effect. In this section we consider how to apply such an analysis to evaluate average delays that arise from multiplexing.

It is well known that a GI/G/1 model can be used to evaluate multiplexing characteristics if the input sequences are uncorrelated [10]. According to the queuing theory, the average delay arising from multiplexing can be approximated as

$$E[B] = \frac{uC^2g}{2(1 - u)} \tag{4.16}$$

$$g = \exp\left\{\frac{-2(1 - u)(1 - C^2)^2}{3uC^2}\right\} \tag{4.17}$$

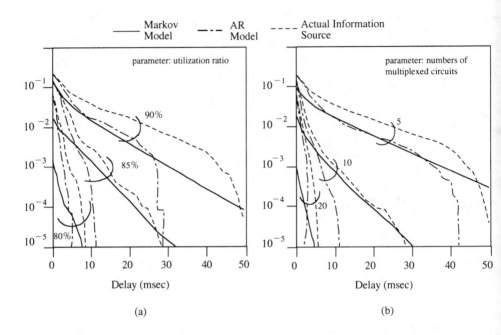

Figure 4.13 Comparison of delay characteristics for (a) ten multiplexed video sources at varying utilization ratios and (b) a fixed utilization ratio of 85% with varying numbers of multiplexed video sources. (Model based on the video signal characteristics of scene (b) encoded by the MC + DCT algorithm.)

Here, $E[B]$ is the average value of the volume of information accumulated in the buffer, u is the utilization ratio, and C is the ratio of the standard deviation to the average value of the bit-rate variability of the information sources. The average delay is obtained by dividing $E[B]$ by the transmission speed, that is, the rate at which data is read out of the buffer.

Since actual video signals obviously exhibit temporal correlations, this method underestimates the delay. This is because a sequence with temporal correlations behaves as a sequence with a large C (the ratio of the standard deviation to the average) when buffered. Recall that the coefficient of variation $C(m)$ was introduced in the previous chapter as a means of evaluating the ratio of standard deviation to average of a buffered sequence. Perhaps the delay times of correlated video signals can be evaluated by substituting $C(m)$ (which is valid for sequences with correlations) for C (which is used for sequences without correlations) in the equation. However, how to deal with the value of m in $C(m)$ is an important issue: we would like to use different values of m to reflect the extent to which the buffer is filled. In general, although evaluation is possible using $C(0)$ when the utilization ratio is low, we want to use $\max[C(m)]$ when the utilization ratio is high. We should be able to evaluate the lower and upper limits of the average delay by using $C(0)$ and $\max[C(m)]$, respectively.

Figure 4.14 shows average delay evaluated using the coefficient of variation. Again, the data is from scene (a), encoded with the MC + DCT algorithm. The measured values

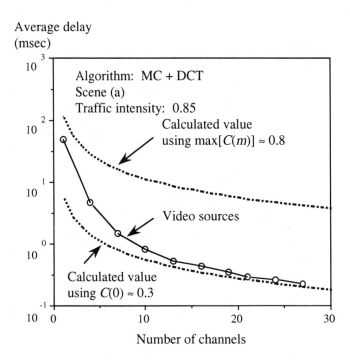

Figure 4.14 Average delay evaluation using the coefficient of variation C(*m*).

for the coefficient of variation presented in Chapter 3 ($C(0) = 0.3$, $\max[C(m)] = 0.8$) were used. As the figure shows, the average delay derived by simulating the multiplexing of actual video signals falls between the upper and lower limits for the delay estimated using coefficients of variation. In regions where the number of multiplexed channels is small and the delay large, the average delay lies close to the upper limit estimated using coefficients of variation, and as the number of multiplexed channels increases, it asymptotically approaches the estimated lower limit. The inverse approach, that is, deriving the coefficient of variation in (4.13) and (4.14) from the average delays obtained by simulation, is shown in Figure 4.15. The results indicate that average delay can be evaluated using $C(0)$ when the utilization does not exceed 0.8 and the number of multiplexed channels is 10 or more. This is identical to the result obtained for AR models in the preceding section. Although the average delay alone does not suffice to fully characterize multiplexing characteristics, these results show that simple evaluation is possible based on the coefficient of variation.

4.4 MODELING SCENE CHANGES

The previous section discussed models based on the assumption that video bit-rate variations are basically continuous and have temporal correlations. However, video signals in

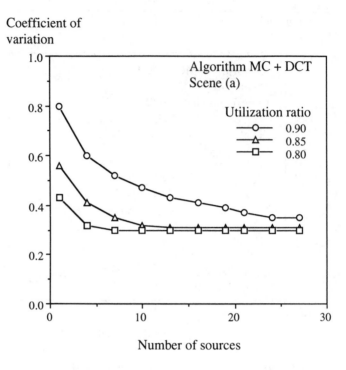

Coefficient of
variation

Figure 4.15 Coefficient of variation calculated from a given average delay.

general, especially TV and movies, include discontinuities due to scene changes. Here, we introduce modeling approaches that focus on scene changes.

A scene change is a transition from one scene to another. If each scene is associated with a process, then a scene change can be seen as a transition between processes. If we assume that the intrascene variations of a single video source can be approximated by a Markov or AR process (short-term variation models), then it might be possible to approximate video signal long-term bit-rate variations by changing the short-term model parameters with a Markov chain. This can be represented generally by a layered model like the model shown in Figure 4.16. In practice, since the variations within a scene are small compared to those resulting from a scene change, the intrascene variations can be ignored. This assumption simplifies modeling and is useful for a simple evaluation of multiplexing characteristics.

4.4.1 Simple Scene Change Modeling for a Single Video Source

In this section we consider an extremely simple model for a single video source that focuses only on scene changes. It is based on the following assumptions:

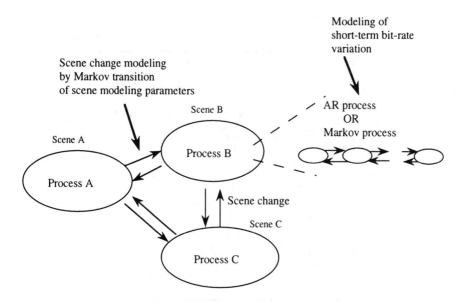

Figure 4.16 Bit-rate-variability modeling that includes scene changes.

1. Scene changes occur independently, and the time between scene changes can be approximated by an exponential.
2. The bit rate within a scene is taken to be fixed, and the bit rate is selected randomly for each scene according to some distribution. For each scene, a random value is chosen based on a certain probability distribution at each scene change. A probability distribution identical to the bit-rate distribution of Figure 3.10, which was obtained from actual video signals, is assumed.

Figure 4.17 shows the effect of statistical multiplexing as simulated by model 1. Here, broadcast television is considered as the video information source; the average bit rate is 9.5 Mbps, standard deviation is 4.2 Mbps, and the maximum rate is 26.4 Mbps. Based on results from the previous chapter, the average scene duration was taken to be 10 sec. The simulation indicates that when 10 video channels are multiplexed, the probability that the total bit rate will exceed 140 Mbps is less than 10^{-6}. The utilization (the average bit rate multiplied by the number of channels and divided by the channel capacity) is about 0.7. Similarly, this figure shows that 50 channels can be multiplexed over a 600-Mbps channel with a utilization of 0.79. As before, the probability that the total bit rate will exceed the channel capacity is below 10^{-6}. This result makes very clear the effectiveness of statistical multiplexing.

How do these results compare to Verbiest's measurements of statistical multiplexing [11]? Verbiest's measurements of seven multiplexed broadcast video sources with an average bit rate of 18.4 Mbps found that the sources could be multiplexed at a utilization of 0.75 with the probability of the total bit rate exceeding the channel capacity being less

Probability

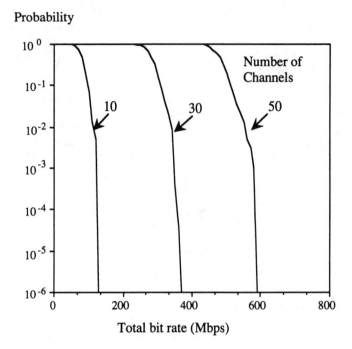

Figure 4.17 Bit-rate distribution of multiplexed video.

than 10^{-7}. Although the scene change model discussed above gives a similar result, it is not meaningful to make numerical comparisons of the statistical multiplexing characteristics because the simple scene change model ignores intrascene bit-rate variations, making accurate comparison problematic.

Durations of Periods of Buffer Overflow

We have seen that a simple evaluation of multiplexing characteristics is possible even if the bit-rate distributions of the individual video sources are approximated by normal distributions. Behavior during buffer overflow, when video signals that include radical rate changes due to scene changes are multiplexed, is a characteristic that can be investigated by simulations based on a scene change model.

In an actual system, congestion will occur with a small but nonzero probability, even if the system design is based on a correct evaluation of statistical multiplexing characteristics using a valid model and a further safety margin is provided. Since congestion in video multiplexing is due to video signal activity, once congestion occurs, it can be expected to continue for an extended period, on the order of the scene length, that is, several seconds. We used scene change model 1 in a simulation to determine how long congestion might continue. We assumed a channel capacity of 600 Mbps, and 50 channels were multiplexed, each of which carries the same video signals, as in Figure 4.17. Actual systems incorporate some method for limiting input prior to buffer overflow and thus preventing overflow. For example, one method is to discard input packets at a certain rate when buffer fullness exceeds a certain level. Therefore, the buffer input control algorithm must be established to accurately simulate the conditions associated with buffer overflow. Here, we attempt a simple estimate by simulating the duration of overflow when video signals are multiplexed. We set the initial bit rate (at time zero) of each video signal to 15 Mbps, and thereafter allow each video signal to vary independently according to the model. This simulation assumes that buffer overflow has already occurred at time zero. When the number of bits arriving per unit time exceeds the volume of data read out per unit time (the constant value C), the excess is discarded and the buffer remains full. When the number of bits arriving per unit time is less than C, space becomes available in the buffer. We investigated the time required for the buffer to reach steady state from time zero. Figure 4.18 shows the results of the simulation. It takes about 10 sec for the congestion occurring at time 0 to be eliminated and for the buffer to return to the normal condition. When congestion occurs, the multiplexing node is forced to discard packets continuously, and unless some provision is made for this situation, a major quality degradation will result. Thus some sort of congestion handling technique must be included either in the network or in the terminal, making congestion-handling signal processing algorithms an extremely important topic for research.

Note that while the average peak length discussed in Chapter 3 was the length of peaks in the smoothly changing bit rates within a single scene, in this section we are concerned with evaluating the duration of high-activity scenes. The characteristics of these aspects of video signals differ.

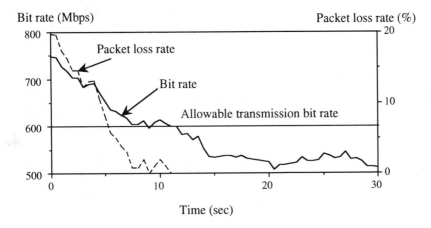

Figure 4.18 Traffic congestion example (50 channels multiplexed over a 600 Mbps transmission line).

4.4.2 Scene Change Modeling Using the Markov Process Model

Using a Markov model, it is possible to approximate the variations within a single scene more precisely than with the model described earlier. Sen et al. extended Maglaris' Markov model in order to model a broader range of video sources, including broadcast television, TV telephone video with scene changes, and teleconferencing video. From the standpoint of correlations, their approach corresponds to taking both short-term and long-term correlations into consideration. Here, we briefly describe the basis of their approach.

In the Maglaris model, the influence of the discrete packet length is ignored, and the data is handled as a continuous bit stream or flow. The reason for this is that while the packet length is on the order of a few dozen bytes, the data rate ranges from 50 Kbps to several megabits per second, and it is assumed that the effects of packetization can be ignored. Since the bit rate is even higher for video that includes scene changes, the same assumption holds here also. Therefore, it is possible to posit statistical multiplexing in a system like that shown in Figure 4.1, with a common buffer (viewed as a fluid-flow pipe) and a prebuffer.

The model proposed by Sen et al. is constructed from a combination of two basic rates, a high rate A_h, and a low rate A_l. A_l corresponds to parameter A in the Maglaris Markov model for a single scene (Figure 4.9). This supposes a video with two types of scenes, scenes with violent motions and scenes with gentle motions. Figure 4.19 shows a Sen model for this type of video. Here, scenes with slow motions have rate variations based on A_l, and scenes with larger motions have rate variations based on A_h.

The model parameters are determined as follows. (This discussion is based on the example in Figure 4.19.) Let $c{:}d$ be the ratio of the time spent at the high activity level (A_h) to the average time spent at the low level (A_l). The high activity level ratio (q) is derived from measurements of actual video signals as $q = c/(c + d)$. The video's overall average bit rate (λ_{all}), the mean ratio γ (the ratio of the average bit rate in the high level to that of the low level), and the autocovariances $C(0)$ and $C(\tau)$ are given by

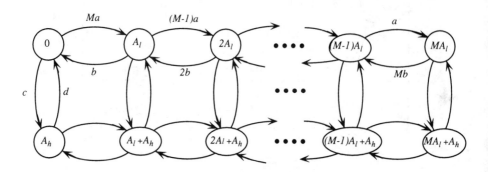

Figure 4.19 State-transition-rate diagram for a two-activity-level source model. (After [12].)

$$\lambda_{all} = MpA_l + qA_h \tag{4.18a}$$

where

$$p = a/(a + b) \tag{4.18b}$$

$$\gamma = (MpA_l + A_h)/MpA_l \tag{4.19}$$

$$C(0) = Mp(1 - p)A_l^2 \tag{4.20}$$

$$C(\tau) = C(0) \exp(-(a + b)\tau) \tag{4.21}$$

Here, the remaining free parameter is M, the number of bit-rate quantization levels.

If a single video source is modeled in this manner, the bit rate when multiple information sources are multiplexed can modeled with the same structure. Thus the multiplexing of N video sources can be modeled with a state-transition-rate diagram like that shown in Figure 4.20. (Note that the rows and columns of Figure 4.19 have been reversed in this figure.)

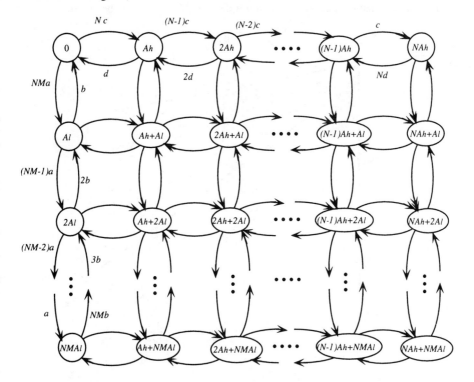

Figure 4.20 State-transmission-rate diagram for the aggregate source model. (N video sources multiplexed.) (After [12].)

Multiplexing characteristics are analyzed with this sort of model in a manner similar to that used in Section 4.3, that is, as the superposition of on/off minisources. For details the reader is referred to [12, p. 867], but the result is that a "survivor function" similar to that of Section 4.3 can be inferred.

Here, we present the results of an analysis of multiplexing assuming videos with two activity levels, such as those shown in Figure 4.19. For example, teleconferencing videos that switch between group scenes (low activity) and close-up scenes of people talking and gesturing (high activity) can be seen as close to this model. Assuming an average bit rate of 3.9 Mbps and equal periods of low and high activity ($c = d$), a loss probability similar to that shown in Figure 4.21 can be derived. This result indicates that a large multiplexing effect can be expected.

4.4.3 Scene Change Modeling Using the Markov Modulated Poisson Process Model

The Markov Modulated Poisson Process Model (MMPP) used by Heffes et. al. in the analysis of packetized voice and data multiplexing [13] can also be applied to video

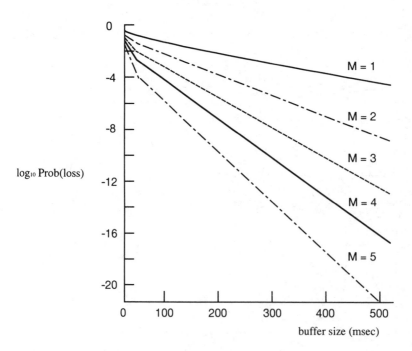

Figure 4.21 Variation of loss probability with buffer size for a utilization of 65% and a mean ratio of 1.5. (After [12].)

signals for a more detailed analysis of the characteristics of large-scale networks. That is, the packet arrival of video signals that include scene changes can be simulated by assuming that packet arrival follows a Poisson process, and the arrival rate varies according to a Markov chain. Yamada [14] modeled such signals under the following assumptions (see Figure 4.22):

1. A single scene is viewed as a single process that generates packets as a Poisson process.
2. The interscene rate transitions are given by a Markov chain.
3. The high bit rate immediately following a scene change is considered to be due either to a high-level state or to clumped arrivals.

The significant feature of Yamada's model is that it attempts to model the rapid increase in bit rate that occurs at a scene change.

These methods might be used for modeling spike-shaped increases in bit rate.

(a) A model based on high-level states that follow Poisson arrival, with extremely high arrival ratios;
(b) A model based on first-order group arrival;
(c) A model based on high-level states with group Poisson arrival.

All these models view bit-rate variations as changes in the number of packet arrivals. Furthermore, for ease of analysis, all distributions (the scene change interval and high-level-state persistence-time distributions) are assumed to be exponential distributions.

The parameters required by these models include the average scene change interval (all models), the average persistence time and arrival ratio of the high-level state (models a and c), and the group size in group arrival (models b and c). Values for these parameters are derived from actual measurements. The average scene change interval can easily be

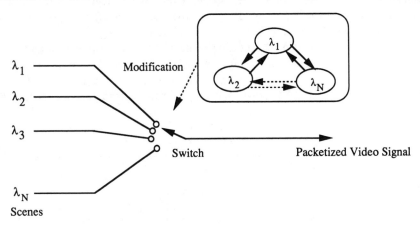

Figure 4.22 Markov modulated Poisson process model for packetized video signals. Assumes either a transition to a Poisson arrival state with an extremely high arrival ratio or a transition clumped arrival.

derived as shown in Chapter 3. From observations of actual bit-rate variations, it is possible to use the minimum unit of encoding processing (normally a single video frame) as a fixed value for the average high-level state persistence time. Given these assumptions, the arrival ratio λ can be derived by matching

$$\lambda \int_0^\infty \mu \exp(-\mu t)dt$$

to the average packet count (i.e., bit rate) in a scene change frame. The group size can be taken to be the arrival packet count in a scene change frame. (However, this value depends on the encoding method.) Finally, the group size I in model c can be derived by matching

$$\lambda_0 \int_0^\infty \mu \exp(-\mu t)dt$$

to the average packet count (i.e., bit rate) in a scene change frame. When the parameters are determined in this way, it is expected that model b will always give a more conservative evaluation. Below, we consider models a and c.

When N independent video sources are multiplexed, the following considerations apply. Since the scene change interval distributions of the various sources were assumed to be exponential distributions, the scene change interval distribution of the multiplexed model will be an exponential distribution with an average scene change interval of $1/N$ of that of a single video source. Models that consider high-level states take one of the N video sources to be in a high-level state, and superpose it on a Poisson process in which the remaining $N - 1$ video sources are varying within scenes. (Intrascene variations are approximated, as they are by Maglaris, as a superposition of on/off minisources. Yamada et. al. used the MMPP method [15].)

Yamada et al. evaluated multiplexing characteristics using models a and c. Their results indicated that although the result of model c was slightly more on the safe side, but the difference was nearly negligible. Table 4.3 shows the video signal bit-rate variation characteristics, and Figure 4.23 shows an example of multiplexing characteristics. Since

Table 4.3
Parameters for MMPP Models

Parameter	Value
Average bit rate	4.5×10^5 (bpf)
Variance	2.1×10^{10} (bpf)
Autocorrelation	$\exp(-ut$: $u = 0.06$ (1/frame)
Average scene length	340 (frame)
Maximum bit rate	1.1×10^6 (bpf)

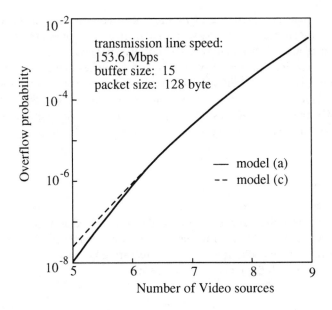

Figure 4.23 Overflow probability versus number of video sources.

in Figure 4.23 the number of video signals multiplexed on a transmission channel whose speed remains fixed is increased, the probability of overflow increases as the number of multiplexed signals increases.

Although we expect that these models can closely approximate the scene change peaks that occur in the variations of actual video signal bit rates, the appropriateness of these models with respect to a variety of video signals, and dependencies on encoding schemes have not yet been confirmed. This remains a problem for future research.

4.4.4 Another Approach

Garrett proposed a method that does not explicitly model scene-dependent structure [16]. As described in Section 3.6.4, he used a Gamma distribution with a Pareto tail and long-range dependence (LRD) to characterize video signals coded with an intraframe DCT-based coding scheme. The distribution is well modeled by a Gamma body with a Pareto tail. This may be described by three parameters: the mean and variance of the Gamma part, plus the exponent giving the hyperbolic rate of decay of the tail. The point where the two meet can be determined by matching the value and first derivative of the Gamma and Pareto parts. The property of LRD indicates that the video process contains events that last a long time, and significantly correlate the bandwidth process for the duration of each event. Such events occur on all time scales, and the longer the duration, the stronger the effect. For example, the last 25% of the movie *Star Wars* contains a trend of increasing action, and therefore increasing mean and variance of bandwidth. Such trends on such a wide variety of time scales are difficult to represent using conventional Markovian source models. In a Markovian model, each parameter signifies a time constant, and the model exhibits random behavior only at frequencies close to those specified. A number of non-Markovian "self-similar" processes exist that capture LRD. A single parameter (H) is used to measure the magnitude of the time correlation. Garrett designed and evaluated a source model for use in computer simulations based on a noise generation process that exhibits long-range dependence and transformation of the marginal distribution [16].

4.5. SUMMARY

Table 4.4 summarizes the *basic* modeling methods described in this chapter. While all these models were proposed to estimate multiplexing characteristics, before actually applying any of these models, it is necessary to carefully consider whether or not the suppositions upon which the model is based hold.

Table 4.4
Basic Video Source Models Summarized

Model	Basis	Method	Video Type	Comments
AR model	Autoregressive model (continuous state)	Simulation	No scene changes (e.g., TV telephone, teleconferencing video with few scene changes)	Closely matches actual video signal characteristics. Accurate evaluation is computationally expensive
Markov model (Maglaris)	Discrete-state, continuous-time Markov model	Analytic	No scene changes (e.g., TV telephone, teleconferencing video with few scene changes)	Closely matches actual video signal characteristics
Markov model (Sen)	Discrete-state, continuous-time Markov model	Analytic	Scene changes (e.g., teleconferencing, broadcast video)	Determining model parameters to fit the model to general video sources is difficult
Markov model (Yamada)	Markov-modified Poisson process	Analytic	Both scene changes and rapid-bit-rate increases generated at scene changes (e.g., teleconferencing, broadcast video)	Further research is required to determine the validity of this model, since, e.g., the peak values of bit rates at scene changes depend on the encoding scheme

Unlike voice signals, which can be explicitly modeled, no general conclusion can be made the validity of any particular video signal model. In TV telephone and teleconferencing video, where the characteristics of the subject videos can be limited to some degree, the models discussed in this chapter are highly applicable. The AR model allows multiplexing characteristics to be easily simulated, and Maglaris' model provides an analytic technique. Thus these models are effective techniques for designing systems that transmit restricted types of video signals, such as teleconferencing and TV telephony.

However, it is not possible to place restrictions on video signals when designing ATM-based CATV transmission systems or when attempting to evaluate the network characteristics of ATM-based B-ISDN for video signals. A general model for unrestricted video sources has not yet been established. Although it is possible to consider extending the model of Figure 4.16 to a general layered model such as shown in Figure 4.24, determining the model parameters is in general very problematic. This is because although it is comparatively easy to create a model for short-term variations for certain limited

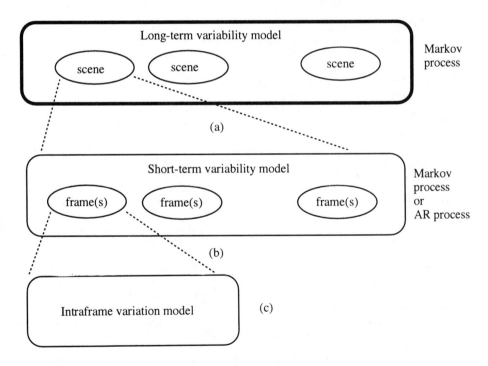

Figure 4.24 Generalized layered modeling of bit-rate variability including scene changes. (a) The long-term variability model, for which bit-rate distribution and average scene duration are matched to the characteristics of actual video sources; (b) the short-term variability model, for which average bit rate, variance, and the autocorrelation function are matched to the characteristics of actual video sources; and (c) the intraframe variation model, which is still an open problem.

types of video, it is difficult to characterize unrestricted video signals that are aggregates of such video signals.

Determining how much channel capacity to provide for an expected traffic level is an important problem in network and system design, and in addition to the modeling issues discussed, there is also the related issue of what sort of controls to apply to the information volume generated and delivered to the network for transmission by individual sources. Furthermore, limitations on the bit rate delivered to the user from the network at the user interface will also have a large influence on design of high-speed packet and ATM networks. However, without an a priori information generation model of the information sources, such limitations cannot be established. Chapters 3 and 4 of this book provide a good starting point for determining the basic characteristics of video signals upon which those limitations must be based. Technological issues associated with traffic management are discussed in Chapter 7.

REFERENCES

[1] Stern, T. E., "A Queuing Analysis of Packet Voice," *Proc. IEEE GLOBECOM '83*, Dec. 1983, pp. 71–76.

[2] Maglaris, B., Anastassiou, D., Sen, P., Karlsson G., and Robbins, J. D., "Performance Models of Statistical Multiplexing in Packet Video Communications," *IEEE Trans. on Comm.*, Vol. 36, No. 7, July 1988, pp. 834–844.

[3] Yasuda, Y., Yasuda, H., Ohta, N., and Kishino, F., "Packet Video Transmission Through ATM Networks," *Proc. GLOBECOM '89*, Dec. 1989, pp. 876–880.

[4] Nomura, M., Fujii, T., and Ohta, N., "Bursty Information Characteristics and Modeling of a Variable Rate Video Coding," *Transaction of IEICE (Institute of Electronics, Information and Communication Engineers)*, Japan, Vol. J71-A, No. 2, Feb. 1988, p. 432 (in Japanese).

[5] Kuriacose, J., et al., "Shared Access Packet Transmission Systems for Compressed Digital Video," *IEEE J. on Selected Areas in Comm.*, Vol. 7, No. 5, June 1989, pp. 815–825.

[6] Huang, S-S, "Source Modeling for Packet Video," *Proc. ICC '88*, June 1988, pp. 1262–1267.

[7] Huang, S-S, "Modeling and Analysis for Packet Video," *Proc. GLOBECOM '89*, Nov. 1989, pp. 881–885.

[8] Anick, D., Mitra, D., and Sondi, M. M., "Stochastic Theory of a Data-Handling System with Multiple Sources," *Bell Syst. Tech. J.*, Vol. 61, No. 8, Oct. 1982, pp. 1871–1894.

[9] Daigle, J. N., and Langford, J. D., "Models of Analysis of Packet Voice Communications Systems," *IEEE J. on Selected Areas in Comm.*, Vol. SAC-4, Sept. 1986, pp. 847–855.

[10] Kleinrock, L., *Queuing Systems*, Vol. 1, New York: Wiley, 1975.

[11] Verbiest, W., Pinnoo, L., and Voeten, B., "Statistical Multiplexing of Variable Bit Rate Video Sources in Asynchronous Transfer Mode Networks," *Proc. GLOBECOM '88*, Dec. 1988, pp. 208–213.

[12] Sen, P., Maglaris, M., Rikli, N., and Anastassiou, D., "Models for Packet Switching of Variable Bit-Rate Video Sources," *IEEE J. Select Areas in Comm.*, Vol. 7, No. 5, June 1989, pp. 865–869.

[13] Heffes, H., and Lucantoni, D. M., "A Markov Modulated Characterization of Packetized Voice and Data Traffic and Related Statistical Multiplexer Performance," *IEEE J. on Selected Areas in Comm.*, Vol. SAC-4, No. 6, Sept. 1986, pp. 856–868.

[14] Yamada, H., "Modeling of Arrival Process of Packetized Video and Related Statistical Multiplexer Performance," (in Japanese), *Technical Report of IEICE*, Japan, IN89-72, 1989, pp. 19–24.

[15] Yamada, H., and Machihara, F., "Analysis of Queuing Model with Phase Type Markov Renewal Input," *Trans. IEICE*, Japan, 1989.

[16] Garrett, M., "Contributions Toward Real-time Services on Packet Switched Networks," Ph.D. Dissertation, Columbia University, 1993, Chapter 4.

Chapter 5
Variable-Rate Video Coding

5.1 INTRODUCTION

In this book, the term *variable-rate video coding* refers to the technology of encoding video information for transmission at a fixed quality while allowing the bit rate to vary freely within a given range, normally determined by the network. The availability of high-speed variable-rate lines, such as those provided by the ATM networks discussed in Chapter 2, will make this type of scheme practical.

What should be the goal of our investigation of variable-rate transmission of video? Current, fixed-rate coding systems are predicated on a fixed bandwidth, which is established to satisfy the quality requirements of a particular service. The ultimate goal of current fixed-rate coding schemes, then, is to maximize the quality of video signal encoding and decoding at a given bit rate. However, the situation becomes more complex when variable-rate coding is considered. In packet network environments, such as ATM, the network's variable-rate circuit and the variable-rate codec act as a single system to implement variable-rate video transmission; it makes no sense to consider either component in isolation. In principle, variable-rate coding makes it possible to deliver video of fixed quality. We say ''in principle'' because it is very difficult to define a measure of video quality and to guarantee that the measure will remain fixed. What then is the ultimate goal for variable-rate transmission? It is, perhaps, to minimize the cost of the entire transmission system required to achieve a certain desired video quality. However, this is too sweeping a goal, and a formal discussion is not possible without establishing the specifications of the service to be provided. Furthermore, consideration of the cost of the entire network lies outside the scope of this monograph.

In this chapter we focus our discussion on those particulars that affect the design of the coding scheme. We discuss technological issues associated with variable-rate coding schemes and demonstrate the quality improvement that variable-rate coding provides using both theoretical and experimental results.

5.2 OVERVIEW OF A VARIABLE-RATE VIDEO CODING SYSTEM

In general, the following requirements are placed on variable-rate coding schemes. Of course, some of them are the same for continuous-bit-rate coding.

- *High information transmission efficiency.* To realize a given video quality level, the lower the bit rate required, the better. In essence, the bit rate should parallel the activity of the video to maximize the coding efficiency by transmitting only new information.
- *Suitability for variable-rate channels.* Variable-rate circuits will generally be implemented by high-speed packet transmission. Thus encoding and decoding should be robust against bursty information loss and fluctuations in transmission delay times, which are the main faults of packet networks.
- *Suitability for networks.* The scheme must be able to accept rate limits and similar controls imposed by the network.
- *Suitability for services.* The scheme must be able to accept service requests, for example, implementing multiple quality levels by switching the rate.
- *Practicality.* The complexity of algorithms must permit real-time operation and implementation in compact hardware.

These requirements are, of course, quite general. We need to look into functions of variable-rate coding in more detail to discuss technological issues.

5.2.1 Functional Overview

Figure 5.1 gives an overview of the processing associated with video signal encoding, from signal input to packetization. The input signal in the figure is an A/D converted (digitized) video signal. The encoding process can be conceptually divided into three stages: compression, quantization, and entropy encoding. Redundancy is removed in the first stage by a form of signal space transform, such as prediction or orthogonal transform. The resultant signal is requantized, at a smaller number of levels than the original signal. In many systems the first and second stages are handled together. For instance, vector quantization performs both compression and quantization. The third stage uses an efficient code allocation algorithm that does not increase the entropy of the redundancy compressed input signal, that is, entropy encoding. Entropy encoding, also referred to as lossless encoding, is a reversible process. In contrast, the first two stages are irreversible, due to their use of finite word length and quantization. While changes in the encoding rate are fundamentally due to changes in the statistical characteristics of the input video signal, they can be more directly understood as arising from the resulting changes in the quantization bit count or in the code allocation of the entropy encoding. While the bit rate in variable-rate coding is in principle free running, obviously some limits will be imposed by the network, and the encoding process will occasionally be controlled by those limits.

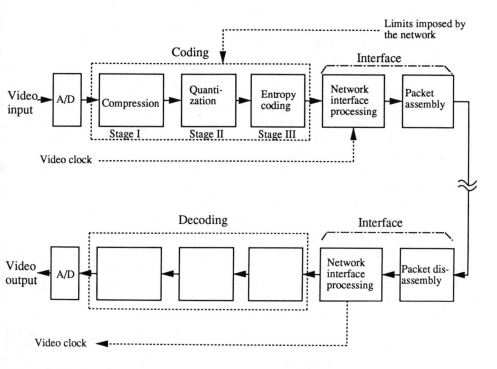

Figure 5.1 Functional description of variable-rate video coding and processing.

After passing through these stages, the compressed video signal is assembled into cells or packets and, after passing through a preprocessing step, is delivered to the network. This preprocessing takes into consideration the features of encoded video signals and the characteristics of networks to reduce the influence of degradation and may include, for example, providing the receiving side with a video synchronization signal to counter the effects of packet transmission jitter (variations in delay).

In order to achieve an end-to-end video communication, such as video/image file transmission between workstations, we need video-transport-level and media-access protocols. We do not discuss such higher level protocols here.

5.2.2 Technological Issues

Having established this overall configuration, the central technological issues can be summarized in these questions.

1. Can quality be improved? How much?

   For a given compression algorithm, how does the quality of variable-rate coding compare with that of fixed rate? It would seem that quality can be increased by increasing the level of freedom of the bit distribution for quantization. Does this effect appear in actual applications?

2. Will new coding algorithms be developed?

When the bit rate is no longer required to be constant, will new coding algorithms be developed? With regard to the basic compression algorithms, the answer is no. Rather, if the compression algorithm is taken to its ultimate limit, the information volume of the compressed signal should vary according to the content of the video input. Therefore, the goals for compression algorithms are fundamentally unchanged. However, as mentioned in Chapters 2 and 3, the organization of those blocks that directly affect the bit volume of the encoded signal, such as the bit distribution of the quantization, changes radically. For instance, the buffer used in fixed-rate encoding to control the bit rate is no longer required, and quantization is determined not so as to fix the rate, but by the criterion that quality is to be maintained at a fixed level. Therefore, control of quantization must be considered in a new light. The entropy encoding stage should be essentially unchanged by the introduction of variable-rate coding, but its measures must be considered to handle the degradation associated with packet loss. Naturally, as we discuss below, these measures will have to take the entire encoding algorithm into account.

3. What error handling measures will be required?

The largest impact on coding algorithms comes from packet loss, the most distinctive characteristic of packet networks. Of course, errors also occur in fixed-rate channels, and video coding algorithms and transmission systems that provide error countermeasures have been proposed before, but error handling was never considered critical. However, error handling is of great importance in variable-rate algorithms for packet network systems. To minimize the influence of errors, more effort should be expended to protect the important parts of the encoded information and to support error recovery or concealment at the decoder. Therefore, there is a need for new, layered algorithms that explicitly address the packet loss phenomenon of packet networks.

4. How will video be synchronized?

Since packet networks introduce delay time jitter, it may be difficult for receiving systems to generate a video terminal synchronization signal simply by extracting it from the video signal, as is done in current systems.

5. What sort of user/network interfaces are needed?

Even with variable-rate encoding, the bit rate is not completely free of limitations. For example, when the network stipulates a peak rate, some form of control is required to assure that the rate does not exceed that limit. Such questions as the form in which limits should be applied by the network, and the best parameters to be stipulated by the network, must be investigated anew.

In this chapter we address the first four of these questions. The last item is discussed in Chapter 7.

5.3. QUALITY IMPROVEMENT BY VARIABLE-RATE CODING

A general discussion of video quality must take into consideration a variety of factors, including spatial and temporal resolution and color reproducibility. In this section we consider the extent to which the quality of a video signal is degraded by the process of encoding, transmission, and decoding. We focus on video of the quality typical of teleconferencing, and compare the effects on quality of fixed-rate and variable-rate encoding [1]. We further limit the discussion to two comparison methods. The first uses the signal-to-noise ratio (SNR), which corresponds to the average power of the magnitude of the pixel distortion due to encoding. The second comparison method employs subjective evaluation. SNR comparisons quantify the influence of spatial resolution, and with certain assumptions it is possible to infer the effect of variable-rate coding by using an analysis based on rate-distortion theory. Subjective comparisons, by including variations in temporal resolution, permit an integrated evaluation not possible with comparisons based only on SNR. In general, temporal effects are not the primary motivation for subjective evaluations. As for telecommunication-type video, there is a sensitive trade-off between space and temporal resolution in controlling coding parameters. Only subjective assessments yield a reasonable video quality comparison in such a case.

Assuming the complete freedom of bit rate, what improvement in quality can be realized by replacing fixed- with variable-rate coding? In practice it is not possible to realize completely arbitrary bit rate encoding since the network will always impose some restrictions, such as a peak-rate limit, but we want to infer the maximum possible quality improvement. The quality improvement is given by comparing the results of fixed- and variable-rate coding of a given video sequence; the total number of bits transmitted is identical in both schemes.

First, we focus on the well-known rate-distortion function for video signal coding. Figure 5.2 shows the general form of the rate-distortion relationships for fixed- and variable-rate coding. The rate-distortion functions in the figure are not necessarily exact; they are intended to illustrate that the function varies with the character of the signal (in particular, the signal distribution and the magnitude of the interframe differences) in approximately the manner shown. With fixed-rate coding, the distortion varies in the range D_1 to D_2 because the rate is held at a fixed value, as shown in (a). With variable-rate coding, the rate varies in the range R_1 to R_2 with variations in the video signal, while the distortion remains fixed, as shown in (b). Similarly, Figure 5.3 demonstrates these relationships as variations over time. In Figure 5.3(a), which illustrates fixed-rate coding, the dotted line indicates the information volume of the video signal itself, which is proportional to the activity of the signal. Since the rate is fixed, when the information content of the signal exceeds the transmission rate, substantial degradation occurs. However, when the rate is permitted to vary in proportion to the information content, as shown in Figure 5.3(b), the quality remains fixed. Figure 5.4 shows typical examples of the rate and SNR distributions for these cases. Here the rate and SNR are totals computed over each frame in the video signal.

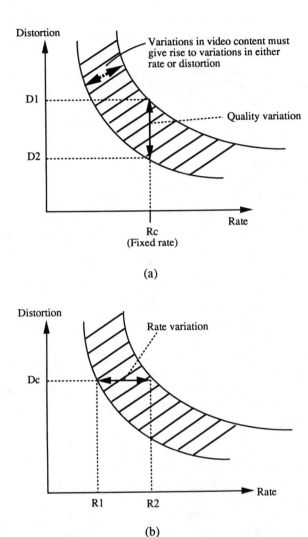

Figure 5.2 Comparison of (a) fixed-rate encoding and (b) variable-rate coding. (Conceptual comparison using the rate-distortion function.)

We can use Figure 5.4 to analyze the improvement in quality that can be expected from variable-rate encoding. For an identical input video signal, equivalent compression and encoding, and the fixed-rate R_C set equal to the average value of the variable-rate R_A, there are two senses in which the quality of variable-rate is higher than that of fixed-rate coding. First, the constant SNR_C for the variable-rate case is higher than the average SNR_A for the fixed-rate case. Second, the coded video with constant SNR that results from

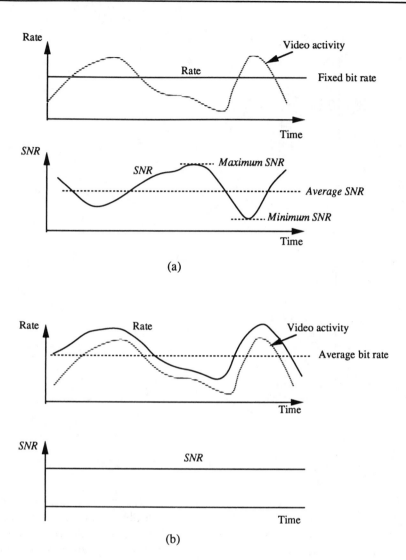

Figure 5.3 Examples of temporal variations in rate and SNR for (a) fixed-rate coding and (b) variable-rate coding.

variable-rate coding is rated as having higher subjective quality than video in which the SNR varies due to a fixed-rate encoding scheme.

The difference between SNR_A and SNR_C depends on the size of the buffer used for fixed-rate encoding. The rate distortion theory shows that the total distortion is minimized when the coded bits are distributed so that distortion is fixed, but fixed-rate encoding can distribute the bits only within a limited range determined by the size of the buffer. In

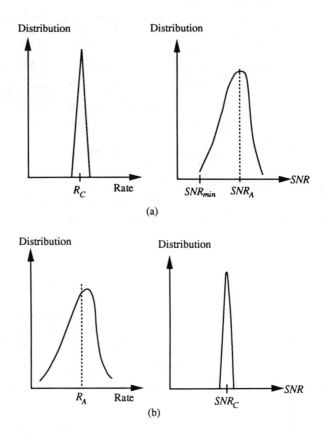

Figure 5.4 Examples of rate and SNR distributions (on a video frame basis) for (a) fixed-rate coding and (b) variable-rate coding.

contrast, ideal variable-rate encoding can distribute the bits optimally. On the other hand, the higher subjective evaluation of video with constant SNR is a reflection not so much of the merits of variable-rate encoding, as of the extreme distortions that occur in fixed-rate encoding. In essence, the low-quality portions of a fixed-rate coded signal influence the perception of the entire video, and the subjective quality of fixed-rate coding is worse than might be expected on the basis of its average SNR.

5.3.1 Estimating Values with the Rate-Distortion Function

Average SNR Improvements

Because ideal variable-rate encoding is equivalent to using an infinite buffer to distribute the encoded bits into a signal stream, it should be possible to increase the average SNR. In this section we investigate the scale of this improvement.

Prediction, transforms, and other techniques are used to remove redundancy from video signals. The signals that result from these algorithms can be viewed ideally as independent random series. However, their distributions will vary depending on the content of the video. The encoding problem can be formulated as follows. Given the total information (the bits) representing the signal series, how should the bits be distributed into each sample?

For an adequately large number of quantization levels, when $R(n)$ bits are distributed over an N element signal series, the mean square distortion D^2 is as follows [1].

$$D^2 = 1/N \sum_{n=0}^{N-1} \sigma^2(n) 2e^{2(\theta - R(n))} \tag{5.1}$$

Here, $\sigma(n)$ is the signal distribution, and θ is a parameter determined by the quantization characteristics and the signal probability density distribution.

The average rate R_A is given by

$$G_{AV} = 10\log_{10}\left\{ \left[1/N \sum_{n=0}^{N-1} \sigma^2(n) \right] \middle/ \left[\prod_{n=0}^{N-1} \sigma^2(n) \right]^{1/N} \right\} \tag{5.2}$$

With the average bit rate set equal to the fixed bit rate R_C, we can minimize the quantization distortion by simply distributing the bits so that the distortion in each sample is constant. If we represent the quantization distortion as D_V, then D_V^2 is given by

$$D_V^2 = \left[\prod_{n=0}^{N-1} \sigma^2(n) \right]^{1/N} 2e^{2(\theta - R_c)} \tag{5.3}$$

On the other hand, if we distribute a constant number of bits into the same series such that the bit rate is R_C, the distortion D_f is given by

$$D_f^2 = 1/N \sum_{n=0}^{N-1} \sigma^2(n) 2e^{2(\theta - R_c)} \tag{5.4}$$

Therefore, we can express the average SNR gain G_{AV} of fixed-rate versus variable-rate coding as the ratio of the arithmetic and geometric means as

$$G_{AV} = 10\log_{10}\left\{ \left[1/N \sum_{n=0}^{N-1} \sigma^2(n) \right] \middle/ \left[\prod_{n=0}^{N-1} \sigma^2(n) \right]^{1/N} \right\} \tag{5.5}$$

The term N in these equations is the unit of bit distribution, and in general, G_{AV} increases as N increases. For typical fixed-rate encoders, N generally corresponds to a buffer that holds one frame, while for ideal variable-rate encoding N is infinite.

Improvement Over Worst-Case Momentary SNR

Here, we consider qualitative measures of the subjective preference for fixed over varying SNR, as discussed earlier in this section. The momentary worst-case quality levels that occur in fixed-rate encoding correspond to SNR_{min} indicated in Figure 5.4. This gives rise to a qualitative degradation that can be expressed approximately as the difference between SNR_C and SNR_{min}. From this standpoint, we define G_{temp} as a measure of the variable-rate encoding gain in regard to momentary quality degradations, using the optimal bit distribution described above. Assuming that fixed-rate encoding uses a buffer the size of a single frame and performs optimum bit distribution over that range, G_{temp} can be expressed as

$$G_{temp} = \min[SNR_V(N,m)] - \min[SNR_V(1,m)] \tag{5.6}$$

Here, $SNR_V(N, m)$ represents the SNR of the mth frame when optimal bit distribution has been performed for N frames as a unit.

Inferring Quality Improvement for Actual Video Signals

In this section we evaluate the variable-rate coding gains G_{AV} and G_{temp}, defined above, for interframe difference signals and for motion-compensated interframe difference signals derived from actual video sources (scene (a) and scene (b) from Chapter 3). Figure 5.5 shows the increase in the average SNR (G_{AV}) and the increase in the worst-case SNR (G_{temp}). The distribution $s(n)$ was determined by evaluating 3×3 pixel areas centered on the pixel in question. Note that this assumes that the fixed-rate encoding uses a one frame buffer, and that optimal bit distribution within a single frame is defined to have a gain of 0 dB.

The diagrams indicate that the improvement in average SNR is small, assuming the fixed-rate encoder uses a one frame buffer; little subjective improvement can be expected. On the other hand, a large improvement in the worst-case SNR can be expected, with G_{temp} on the order of 5–10 dB. That is, it appears that the problem of momentary degradations can be substantially alleviated. In general, the degree of momentary degradation is linked to the activity of the video. In the examples of Figure 5.5, the improvement is larger for scene (a), although this video has less motion. However, this can be explained by the fact that scene (b) includes abrupt camera motions, thus giving results similar to scenes with large subject motions.

5.3.2 Evaluation of SNR Improvement via Simulation

The assumptions of the previous section may not hold in actual encoding, because the number of bits is quite limited and the signal that results from prediction and other compression techniques is not necessarily an independent series. Furthermore, in actual

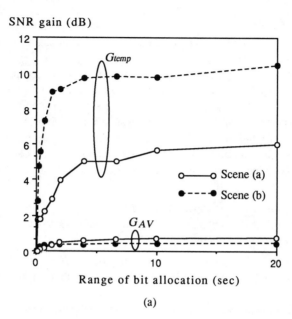

(a)

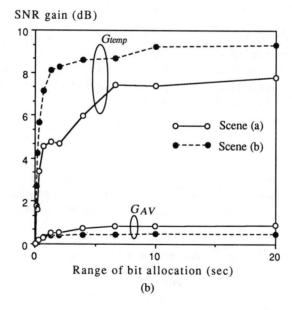

(b)

Figure 5.5 SNR improvement with variable-rate coding for (a) an interframe difference signal and (b) a motion-compensated interframe difference signal. (G_{temp}: improvement in worst-case SNR, G_{AV}: improvement in average SNR.)

encoding it is difficult to accomplish optimal bit distribution. In this section we use simulations to confirm whether the inferred improvements can in fact be obtained in actual variable-rate encoding.

Although it would be possible in the simulation to use for comparison an algorithm that encodes each pixel with a fixed number of bits, most actual encoding algorithms based on interframe coding assume a buffer whose size corresponds to at least a frame of image data. Therefore, we will compare variable-rate coding to a fixed-rate encoder that uses a one-frame buffer as the rate buffer and that adjusts for buffer overflow or underflow by changing the number of bits in the quantization process.

We examine three interframe prediction-based algorithms as the encoding algorithms.

(a) Interframe difference encoding (DPCM);
(b) Interframe difference encoding with motion compensation;
(c) DCT with motion compensation.

These are the same algorithms used in Chapter 3. We expect, from the preceding theoretical discussions, that the quality improvements with these algorithms will not differ in character.

Simulations were performed for the videos used in the previous section, and comparisons of the actual average SNR gain G_{AV} and worst-case SNR gain G_{temp} are shown in Table 5.1.

As expected from the discussion of the previous section, the average SNR is improved less than is the worst-case SNR. At 2–5 dB, however, the increase was rather larger than expected. It may be that momentary SNR degradations lower the prediction efficiency with fixed-rate encoding and, therefore, the average SNR. The improvement in worst-case SNR, at 5–10 dB, is in the expected range.

5.3.3 Subjective Evaluations of Quality

The subjective quality of a video depends not only on the spatial resolution and SNR, but also on the temporal resolution, that is, the frame rate. In particular, the low-bit-rate video encoding used in teleconferencing frequently resorts to reducing the frame rate

Table 5.1
SNR Improvement in Coding Simulation

Algorithm	DPCM		MC + DPCM		MC + DCT	
Scene	1	2	1	2	1	2
Average bit rate (bps)	2.7M	1.7M	2.0M	1.2M	252K	139K
G_{AV} (dB)	3.4	1.6	2.0	1.7	5.1	3.4
G_{temp} (dB)	9.0	7.2	5.0	4.8	10.0	8.2

below the 30 fps used in normal video, giving rise to unnatural motion. Low, fixed-rate encoding typically sacrifices the frame rate during periods of high video activity in order to maintain the spatial resolution. There is a possibility of evaluating this effect by observing SNR variation in time on a frame-by-frame basis. However, there is no general method known for this type of evaluation except subjective evaluation. In the following section, we investigate the overall quality improvements produced by variable-rate encoding, including degradations that cannot be evaluated considering SNR only, and we investigate to what extent the worst-case SNR improvements discussed in the previous section are meaningful as a measure of overall quality improvement.

Encoding Algorithms

With these points in mind, we select MC + DCT as the low-bit-rate encoding algorithm and apply the three encoding control algorithms subsequently described. These are, of course, somewhat artificial methods, introduced only for the purpose of measuring the quality improvement, and they differ from the techniques used in actual encoding equipment.

(a) *Bit rate is fixed by controlling quantization.* The bit rate is evaluated for each video frame, and quantization is controlled to keep the rate at a fixed value. The frame rate is constant.

(b) *Bit rate is fixed by varying the frame rate.* The frame rate is allowed to vary within a certain range, and a one-frame buffer is assumed. The bit rate is held approximately constant by lowering the frame rate whenever the buffer threatens to overflow.

(c) *SNR fixed.* The quantization is controlled to hold SNR, evaluated on a frame basis, constant. The frame rate is constant.

Subjective Evaluation Procedure

We applied these three encoding control schemes to MC + DCT, displayed on a screen the result of encoding at several average bit rates, and evaluated the results. We used a mean opinion score (MOS) as the measure in the subjective evaluations and evaluated each result as a teleconferencing video, on a scale from 1–5. The conditions under which the subjects performed the subjective evaluations are summarized in Table 5.2. Two 5-sec scenes of people conversing (data 1 and data 2) were used as the video signals. In data 1, the subject motions are relatively large, while in data 2 they are relatively small. The frame rate was 15 fps.

Results of Subjective Evaluation

Figure 5.6 shows the results of the subjective evaluations. For constant frame-rate encoding, methods that fix the SNR received an MOS 1–1.5 points higher than those that fix the number of bits per frame. This observation holds for both Data 1 and Data 2. When we

Table 5.2
Subjective Evaluation Procedures

Method	Comparison with Original Data (8b PCM)
Measure	MOS (scale of 1–5)
	(Evaluated as teleconferencing video)
	5: Very good
	4: Good
	3: OK
	2: Poor
	1: Very poor
Viewing conditions	Viewing distance: 6H
	(H = height of screen)
	21″ screen
	29 participants
Video sources	256 × 240 pixels, 15 fps
	5-sec sequences, each viewed twice in succession
	2 sequences with teleconferencing content
	Data 1: Conferees move quite a bit
	Data 2: Conferees move very little

observe the fixed-bit-rate videos, it is clear that the SNR degradation in frames with larger subject motion is responsible for the lower evaluations.

It is interesting to compare the evaluation of video in which the frame rate is varied to fix the bit rate with that in which the bit rate is varied to fix the SNR. Data 1, which has larger motion, received an MOS about 0.5 points higher for fixed SNR coding than for fixed-bit-rate coding. For Data 2, however, there was almost no difference. This may be because the degradation due to reductions in the frame rate is not particularly noticeable in video, such as Data 2, where the motions are relatively limited.

To get a more precise comparison of variable frame rate, fixed-bit-rate control versus fixed-SNR control, we had subjects compare the two results for Data 2 only. Approximately 70% of our subjects preferred the video resulting from fixed-SNR control. In general, it is extremely difficult to determine how to balance image SNR and video motion smoothness to maximize the subjective evaluation. However, these results indicate that blithely reducing the frame rate is quite likely to result in a lower subjective quality, and that variable-bit-rate, fixed-SNR encoding can be used to increase quality. If, for example, video that contains sections of extremely little motion is to be variable-rate encoded, it may be possible to aggressively adjust the frame rate to accomplish low-bit-rate encoding without sacrificing quality, but this should be considered only as an extension to variable-rate, fixed-SNR coding [2].

Subjective Measures for Quality Improvement via Variable-Rate Encoding

These results seem to indicate that momentary degradations influence the overall subjective evaluation of an video. Therefore, when considering comparisons of variable- and fixed-

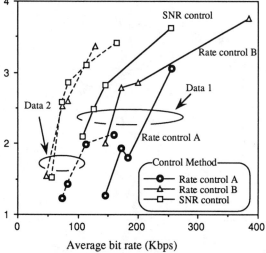

Mean Opinion Score (MOS)

Average bit rate (Kbps)

Rate control A: fixed bit rate, fixed frame rate
Rate cotnrol B: fixed bit rate, variable frame rate
Data 1: large motion
Date 2: little motion

Figure 5.6 Subjective quality improvement obtained by quality control. Rate control A: fixed bit rate, fixed frame rate; rate control B: fixed bit rate, variable frame rate; data 1: large motion; data 2: little motion.

rate encoding quality, we need evaluation measures that take account of momentary degradations. One such measure might be the smallest value, in a particular video sequence, of the moving average of the SNR of each frame. This worst-case value, SNR_{min}, can be defined as

$$SNR_{min} = \min_{(j)} \left[\sum_{i=j}^{j+L-1} SNR_f(i)/L \right] \qquad (5.7)$$

Here $SNR_f(i)$ is the SNR of the ith frame, and L is the range over which the moving average is calculated. That is, L expresses the time scale for the worst-case value evaluation.

We can infer an appropriate value for the parameter L from the subjective evaluation results presented above. We calculated the SNR_{min} for the encoded videos used in the subjective evaluations. Figure 5.7 shows the correlation of SNR_{min} with the subjective evaluation (MOS) for various time scales, and indicates that a value of about 8 is appropriate for L, both for video with large motion and with smaller motion. Figure 5.8 compares MOS evaluations with SNR_{min} when L is 8. Since the relationship is essentially linear, SNR_{min} would seem to be a useful measure of quality.

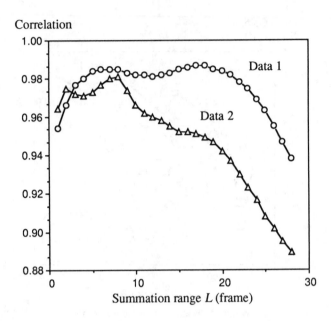

Figure 5.7 Correlation between $SNR_{\min}$ and MOS under various summation ranges.

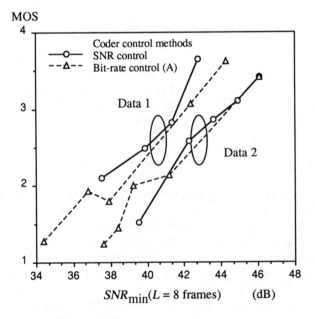

Figure 5.8 Relation between $SNR_{\min}$ and MOS.

5.4 SIGNAL PROCESSING IN VARIABLE-RATE CODING

This section discusses signal processing techniques for compression, control of output rate and video quality, and architecture of variable-rate coding schemes. We omit the details of the algorithms and cover only the basic principles.

5.4.1 Fundamental Compression Algorithms

Predictive Coding

Prediction is probably the most fundamental compression method (for any signal, not only those carrying video information). The basis of predictive encoding is to reduce the bit rate by taking advantage of correlations in the input signal. Video signals exhibit correlations both between pixels within a frame (spatial correlations) and between pixels in differing frames (temporal correlations). The spatial correlations are exploited by intraframe prediction methods, while interframe prediction techniques take advantage of the temporal correlation. Hybrid methods use a combination of these methods. Because interlaced video scans alternate lines to distribute the pixels of a single frame across two fields, it is amenable also to intra and interfield prediction methods.

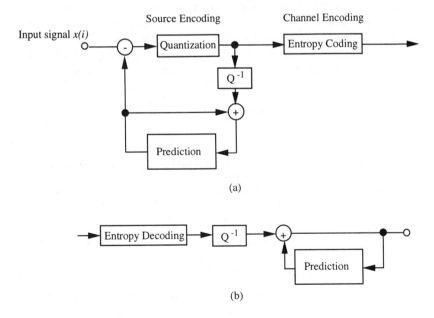

Figure 5.9 Basic structure of predictive coding: (a) the encoder and (b) the decoder.

Figure 5.9 illustrates the basic principles of predictive encoding schemes. The input signal $x(i)$ consists of digitized pixels. Compression is performed by quantizing the difference between the input signal and the predicted value. The compression and quantization stages of Figure 5.1 have been combined here to form the block labeled "source encoding." If the prediction is good, then the differences, or residuals, will be distributed in a small range centered on 0 and can be quantized with a small number of bits. The performance of predictive encoding, then, is determined by the quality of the prediction. Table 5.3 lists examples of prediction functions. The internal complexity of the predictor (the block labeled "prediction" in the figure) varies with the prediction function. Interfield prediction requires memory to hold a single field, and interframe requires memory to hold a single frame. Motion compensation, one of the most complex prediction methods, reduces the prediction error by predicting the motion of the imaged objects.

A weakness of prediction-based encoding is that the influence of any errors during data transmission affects all subsequent data. In particular, when interframe prediction is used, the influence of transmission errors is quite noticeable. Since predictive encoding schemes are often used in combination with other schemes, such as transform-based schemes, the influence of transmission errors must be given due consideration.

Transform Coding

If we consider the frequency distribution of signals containing strong correlations, it is apparent that the signal power is concentrated in the low-frequency region. In general, it should be possible to exploit for compression any systematic bias in components of the signal. The basic idea behind transform coding is to transform the original signal in such a way as to emphasize the bias, making it more amenable to techniques that remove

Table 5.3

Examples of Prediction Functions

Prediction Type	Functions
Intrafield	*Previous value:* uses value of spatially adjacent pixel on same line
	Single line: uses value of pixel on previous line
	Average value: uses average of values of adjacent pixel on same line and on previous line
Interfield	*Average value:* uses average of values of pixel in same position in previous field and its adjacent pixels
Interframe	*Interframe previous value:* uses value of pixel in corresponding position in previous frame
	Motion compensation: computes motion vectors and predicts assuming that pixels in previous frame move according to motion vectors

redundancy. A number of orthogonal transforms, including the discrete Fourier transform and the discrete cosine transform (DCT) have been used. Of these transforms, DCT is most widely used because the power of the transformed signal is well concentrated in the low frequencies, and it can be computed rapidly [3].

The following expresses a 2-dimensional DCT for an $N \times N$ pixel block.

$$X(u, v) = \frac{4C(u)C(v)}{N^2}\sum_{j=0}^{N-1}\sum_{k=0}^{N-1}x(j, k)\cos\left(\frac{(2j + 1)u\pi}{2N}\right)\cos\left(\frac{(2k + 1)v\pi}{2N}\right) \qquad (5.8)$$

$$x(j, k) = \sum_{u=0}^{N-1}\sum_{v=0}^{N-1}C(u)C(v)X(u, v)\cos\left[\frac{(2j + 1)u\pi}{2N}\right]\cos\left[\frac{(2k + 1)v\pi}{2N}\right] \qquad (5.9)$$

where

$$C(w) = \begin{cases} \dfrac{1}{\sqrt{2}} & w = 0 \\ 1 & w = 1, 2, \ldots, N - 1 \end{cases} \qquad (5.10)$$

Larger values of N improve the SNR, but the effect saturates above a certain block size. Further, increasing the block size increases the total computation cost required. The value of N is thus chosen to balance the efficiency of the transform and its computation cost; block sizes of 8–16 are common [3].

The encoding of the transformed coefficients $X(u,v)$ takes into account both their statistical characteristics and their visual significance. For example, consider the 8×8 DCT-transformed coefficients plotted as two-dimensional frequencies in Figure 5.10. $X(0,0)$ expresses the DC component, which is the average value of the corresponding pixel block, while the horizontal axis shows the frequencies in the horizontal direction,

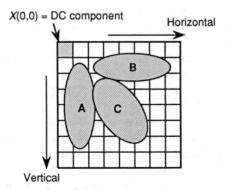

Figure 5.10 DCT-transformed coefficients.

and the vertical axis shows the frequencies in the vertical direction. The coefficient $X(0,0)$ is more visually significant than the other transformed coefficients. That is, if the DC component is quantized at low resolution, the brightness of each block will differ from that of the original signal, resulting in visually distracting block distortion. Therefore, a large number of bits is usually allocated for $X(0,0)$, and linear uniform quantization applied. Various techniques are applied to the other coefficients to reduce the bit rate. The basic idea is that more bits are allocated to regions where the signal power is concentrated. For example, if there is a vertical edge in the original image, there will be a concentration of coefficients with large absolute values in the region marked A in Figure 5.10. Similarly, coefficients with relatively large values will be distributed in the region marked B for a vertical edge and in the region marked C for a diagonal edge. Schemes that efficiently code-transformed coefficients with priorities that differ according to aspects of the image have proved to be of practical value. These coding schemes are described in detail in [3] and other references.

In practice, DCT is used in conjunction with other techniques, such as prediction and subband coding. The MC + DCT scheme, which we have repeatedly referred to, is a prime example of such a combination.

Subband Coding

Subband coding refers to the compression methods that divide the signal into multiple bands to take advantage of a bias in the frequency spectrum of the video signal. That is, efficient encoding is performed by partitioning the signal into multiple bands and taking into account the statistical characteristics and visual significance of each band. Still images are amenable to 2-dimensional, and moving images to 3-dimensional subband coding. Broadly speaking, the transform coding schemes discussed in the previous section can be considered instances of subband coding.

The general form of a subband coding system is shown in Figure 5.11. In the encoder, the analyzing filters partition the input signal into bands, each band is separately encoded, and the encoded bands are multiplexed and transmitted. The decoder reverses this process. Until recently, prediction and DCT were the principal techniques used for video signal encoding, in part because the analysis into bands required by subband encoding was too computationally expensive for practical implementation. Because separate control of the encoding for each frequency band, which is the principal advantage of subband coding, is also a feature of DCT, the computational expense of subband coding did not seem to be justified. However, subband encoding does offer several advantages. Unlike DCT, it is not prone to block distortion. Only the analyzing and synthesizing filters entail high computational expense, and because the output of the analyzing filters is subsampled, the encoding computation may proceed at a more leisurely pace. For these reasons, researchers in fields such as HDTV, where high-quality, high-speed processing is required, are reevaluating subband coding [4, 5]. Furthermore, subband encoding would seem,

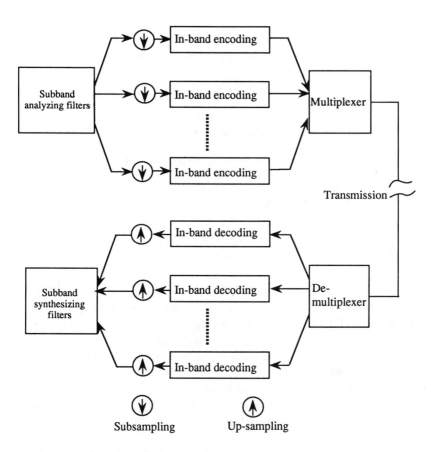

Figure 5.11 Subband coding scheme (basic structure).

intuitively, to be the most natural coding scheme when hierarchical processing is needed for the variable-rate coding scheme, as discussed in Section 6.4.

The main technological features to be determined in subband encoding are the subband analysis method (2- or 3-dimensional), the structure of the analyzing filters, the bit allocation method, and the compression method within each band. In particular, there are quite a number of candidates for the form of the analysis and the structure of the filters. The filters must not introduce distortion due to aliasing in-band analysis and synthesis. The symmetric short-kernel filter has been shown to be more appropriate for video signal subband analysis than the quadrature mirror filter [6] traditionally used in audio signal subband analysis, and is widely used. The advantage of the symmetric short-kernel filter is that the signal can be completely reproduced even if the filter is of low order. In the following discussion we demonstrate the utility of the symmetric short-kernel filter in a simple 2-band subband encoding scheme [7].

Figure 5.12 shows a 2-band analysis and synthesis system. The analyzing filter characteristics shown below might be used for the short-kernel filter bank.

$$H_l(z) = \frac{1}{4}(1 + 2z^{-1} + z^{-2}) \qquad H_h(z) = \frac{1}{4}(-1 - 2z^{-1} + 6z^{-2} - 2z^{-3} - z^{-4}) \qquad (5.11)$$

For these analyzing filters, the characteristics of the synthesizing filters are

$$G_l(z) = H_h(-z) \qquad G_h(z) = H_l(-z) \qquad (5.12)$$

The characteristics of these filters are illustrated in Figure 5.13.
The relationship between the input and output is then

$$Y(z) = \frac{1}{2}[H_l(z)X(z) + H_l(-z)X(-z)]G_l(z) - \frac{1}{2}[H_h(z)X(z) + H_h(-z)X(-z)]G_h(z) = z^{-3}X(z)$$

$$(5.13)$$

Clearly, the aliasing components completely cancel. The basic principles illustrated hold unchanged when 2-dimensional filtering is used in a practical application.

Figure 5.14 illustrates how the 2-dimensional frequency domain may be partitioned either uniformly or in an octave pattern. If we recall that signal power will be concentrated in the low-frequency components, then the octave method (5.14(b)) seems the most natural. Since this corresponds to constructing the analyzing filters in a tree structure, it lends itself well to implementation with filter banks.

Woods [8] collects a number of useful papers on subband coding, and the work is recommended to the reader who wishes to research the topic more thoroughly.

Vector Quantization

As opposed to scalar quantization, in which sample values are independently quantized one at a time, vector quantization (VQ) attempts to remove redundancy between sample

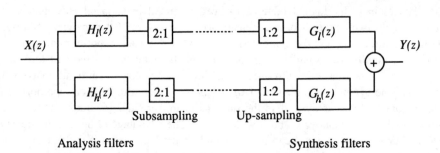

Figure 5.12 Subband coding scheme (2-band system).

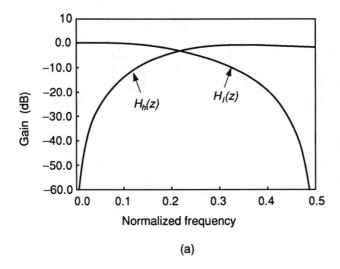

(a)

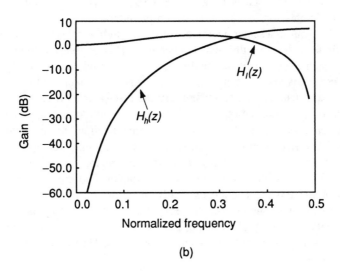

(b)

Figure 5.13 Characteristics of analyzing and synthesizing filters. (a) $H_l(z) = 1/4(1 + 2z^{-1} + z^{-2})$; $H_h(z) = 1/4(-1 - 2z^{-1} + 6z^{-2} - 2z^{-3} - z^{-4})$. (b) $H_l(z) = 1/4(-1 + 3z^{-1} + 3z^{-2} - z^{-3})$; $Hh(z) = 1/4(1 - 3z^{-1} + 3z^{-2} - z^{-3})$.

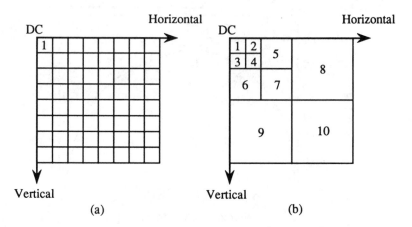

Figure 5.14 Subband splitting patterns in 2-dimensional frequency domain: (a) uniform split (8 × 8), (b) octave split (10).

values by collecting several sample values and quantizing them as a single vector [9,10]. Accordingly, it combines stages 1 and 2 of Figure 5.1. It is also possible to combine this method with compression in stage 1 based on prediction.

Since the input to a scalar quantizer consists of individual sample values, the signal space is a finite interval of the real number line. This interval is divided into several regions, and each region is represented in the quantized outputs by a single value. The input to a vector quantizer is typically an n-dimensional vector, and the signal space is likewise an n-dimensional space. To simplify the discussion, we consider only the case where $n = 2$. In this case, the input to the quantizer is the vector $\mathbf{x_j}$, which corresponds to the pair of samples $(\mathbf{S_j^1}, \mathbf{S_j^2})$. To perform vector quantization, the signal space is divided into a finite number of nonoverlapping regions, and a single vector to represent each region is determined. When the vector $\mathbf{x_j}$ is input, the region containing $\mathbf{x_j}$ is determined, and the representative vector for that region, $\mathbf{y_j}$, is output. This concept is shown in Figure 5.15. If we phrase the explanation explicitly in terms of encoding and decoding, the encoder determines the region to which the input $\mathbf{x_j}$ belongs and outputs j, the index value which represents the region. The decoder receives this value j, extracts the corresponding vector $\mathbf{y_j}$ from the representative vector set, and outputs it. The set of representative vectors is called the *codebook*.

The performance of vector quantization is evaluated in the same manner as for other schemes, that is, by the relationship between the encoding rate and the distortion. The encoding rate R per sample is given by (5.14), where K is the vector dimensionality, and N is the number of quantization levels.

$$R = \lceil \log_2 N \rceil / K \qquad (5.14)$$

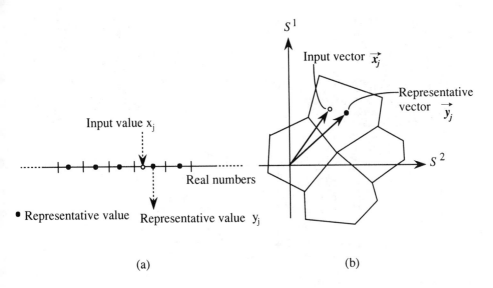

Figure 5.15 (a) Scalar and (b) vector (2-dimensional) quantization.

The notation $\lceil\ \rceil$ represents the smallest integer greater than or equal to x (the "ceiling" of x).

We define the distortion as the distance between the input vector $\mathbf{x}_j$ and the output vector $\mathbf{y}_j$. In video encoding, the square of the Euclidean distance is generally used as a distortion measure because it makes analytic design of the vector quantizer for minimal distortion more tractable. However, it is not necessarily the case that subjective distortion perceived by a human observer coincides with the squared distortion.

To design a high performance vector quantizer, the representative vectors and the regions they cover must be chosen to minimize total distortion. If the input vector probability density function is known in advance, and the vector dimensionality is low, it is possible to perform an exact optimization. However, in an actual application it is rare for the input vector probability density to be known in advance. The well-known *LBG* algorithm is widely used for adaptively designing vector quantizers in this situation [11]. *LBG* is a practical algorithm that starts out with some reasonable codebook, and, by adaptively iterating the determination of regions and representative vectors, converges on a better codebook.

Figure 5.16 shows the basic structure of an image codec based on vector quantization. The image is partitioned into M-pixel blocks, which are presented, one at a time, to the VQ encoder as the M-dimensional vector $\mathbf{x}_j$. The encoder locates the closest representative vector in its prepared codebook and transmits the representative vector's index. The decoder, which need only perform a simple table lookup in the codebook to output the representative vector, is an extremely simple device. The simplicity of the decoder makes VQ coding very attractive for broadcast- and distribution-type video services. However,

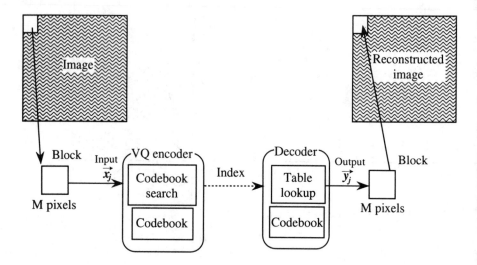

Figure 5.16 Structure of vector-quantizing codec.

VQ coding alone is not an adequate strategy for design of a high-performance system, for two reasons. First, the encoding performance cannot be increased without increasing the vector dimensionality (M), but computation and memory requirements explode as M increases; the practical upper limit is about 16 (4×4 pixel blocks). The second reason is that it is difficult to ensure codebook generality with respect to the input images. A variety of techniques have been used to address these problems. The approach of applying VQ after the video has been transformed to a signal that conforms to some standard distribution is quite common. Combination with orthogonal transformation or other methods is also common.

Entropy Coding

In this section we describe entropy encoding, the third stage in a variable-rate encoder. The preceding encoder stages, described earlier in this chapter, decrease the average rate by removing redundancy from the video signal using such techniques as prediction or orthogonal transformations. Compression in these stages takes advantage of temporal and spatial correlations in the video signal. Entropy encoding, on the other hand, reduces the size of the data sequence by focusing on the statistical characteristics of the encoded data series to allocate efficient codes, independent of the characteristics of the video signal.

The basic concepts of entropy coding are as follows. First, we define the term *information*. Consider a video signal in which each pixel takes on one of K values. If the spatial correlations have been removed from the video signal, the probability that a particular level i appears will be P_i, independent of the spatial position. When such a video signal is transmitted, the information I imparted to the receiver by knowing which of K levels is the value of a particular pixel, is $-\log_2 P_i$ bits. This value, averaged over an image, is referred to as the average information of the image, or the entropy. The entropy can therefore be expressed as

$$H = -\sum_{i=0}^{K-1} P_i \log_2 P_i \tag{5.15}$$

Entropy encoding attempts to perform efficient code allocation (without increasing the entropy) for a signal that has been compressed by prediction or orthogonal transform. Huffman encoding and run-length encoding are well-known basic methods for efficient code allocation, and are commonly used in actual encoders [12,13]. Huffman encoding produces extremely compact codes when the probability distribution P_i is known, while run-length encoding focuses on uninterrupted sequences, or *runs*, of zeros or ones to produce an efficient encoding. We will omit a detailed discussion, but the important point is that when entropy encoding is employed, the information in a signal compressed by prediction or orthogonal transformation is directly reflected in the bit rate. That is, the variations in the entropy generated by changes in the video content, such as subject motion, appear directly as variations in the bit rate. Therefore, the discussions in Chapter 3 assume that entropy encoding is employed.

5.4.2 Examples of Variable-Rate Video Codecs

In this section we introduce the actual variable-rate (VR) codecs and show how they use signal processing techniques. A variety of coding algorithms have been proposed; here, we consider those employing discrete cosine transform, subband, and vector quantization for coding. In particular, we focus our discussion on the signal processing techniques used for compression, control of quality and bit rate in the compression stage, and the differences between variable- and fixed-rate codecs. Packet loss countermeasures, which usually attempt to impose some hierarchical structure on the data, are covered in detail in Chapter 6.

Motion Compensation Plus Discrete Cosine Transform (MC + DCT)

We suppose that the video to be encoded consists of teleconferencing services. For this type of video, motion compensation carried out on the basis of frame differences is quite effective because the imaged subjects engage in limited motions. Motion compensation can be combined with the discrete cosine transform for even more effective compression. The combination is typically referred to as MC + DCT, and was mentioned in Chapter 3, where we considered the burstiness of video signals. Here we outline an MC + DCT-based VR codec in order to gain an understanding of the technological issues.

The overall configuration of MC + DCT is illustrated in Figure 5.17. The block selector compares its input signal with that of the previous frame (generally in units of 8 × 8 pixel blocks) and selects those which exhibit motion. Only those blocks in which motion exceeds a threshold value are selected for encoding. ("MC" in the figure is an abbreviation for motion compensation.) Motion compensation operates by comparing, the input signal in units of blocks against a locally decoded copy of the previous frame, extracting a motion vector and using the motion vector to calculate the frame difference. The motion vector is extracted by, for example, shifting vertically or horizontally a region several pixels on a side and performing matching within the block [14].

The motion-compensated frame-difference signal is then discrete cosine transformed in order to remove spatial redundancy. A variety of compression techniques are applied in quantizing the DCT coefficients; the reader is directed to the references for details [15]. A leading method is zig-zag scan, which has been standardized as H.261 for video transmission encoding [16]. Zig-zag scan, which transforms 2-dimensional data into one dimension, is illustrated in Figure 5.18. Because the DC component of the coefficients is of critical importance, ordinary linear quantization is employed for them. Other components are scanned, in zig-zag fashion, from low to high frequency, linearly quantized

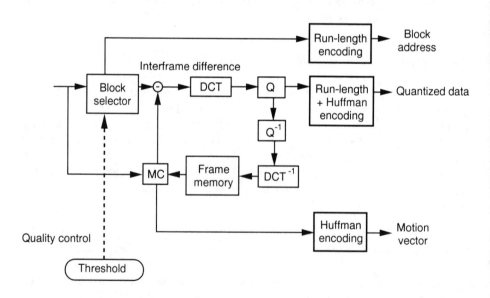

DCT: discrete cosine transform   DCT^{-1}: inverse discrete cosine transform
MC: motion compensation
Q: quantizer (scanning from low to high frequency)

Figure 5.17 Block diagram of variable-rate motion-compensated DCT.

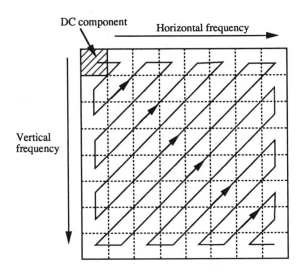

Figure 5.18 Zig-zag scan of DCT coefficients.

with a dead zone, and variable-length-encoded using Huffman or run-length coding. The characteristic function of a quantizer with a dead zone is shown in Figure 5.19.

Controlling Quality

If the pixel count, color signal format, and frame rate of the input signal are fixed, and we ignore for the moment the possibility of packet loss, the elements of an MC + DCT-based VR codec that affect coding quality are

(a) The threshold value used to select blocks to be encoded based on interframe prediction;
(b) The quantization characteristic applied to the transform coefficients (step size and size of the dead zone).

If the motion threshold is reduced, a larger number of blocks on the screen will be encoded and transmitted, resulting in smoother motion of the decoded video and thus improved quality. Manipulating the quantization characteristic function corresponds to manipulating the SNR for each block. In general, decreasing the step size and reducing the dead zone increases the SNR. Naturally, manipulating these quality-control parameters affects the codec's average bit rate. However, because the characteristics of the input video signal cannot be predicted, the parameters cannot be adjusted in such a way as to ensure any particular average rate for the encoded output of the codec.

Figure 5.17 does not make clear how the threshold value, which affects the coding quality, is determined. One possibility is that the codec acts to limit its own output rate

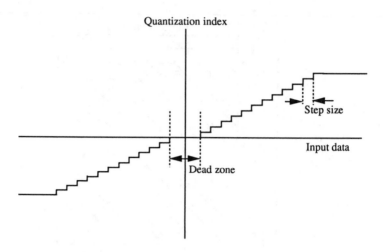

Figure 5.19 Linear quantization with dead zone.

at the request of the user/network interface when a monitor function of the network determines that discipline is in order.

Quality and Rate Variability

Figure 5.20 shows an example of SNR and encoded bit rate for an actual video signal sequence encoded with MC + DCT. The video format is 256 × 240 pixels at 15 fps, and the imaged subject is a person. The SNR and bit rate (in bps) were measured for each frame. The SNR is approximately constant, but small variations do arise because the prediction residuals vary with the motion of the image. The figure also shows the SNR for a fixed-rate encoder which uses the same compression method and a rate buffer to control the quantization characteristic function. The poor SNR of the first half of the video sequence is due to the imaged subject moving around while holding some documents, resulting in large motion signals. Figures 5.21 and 5.22 illustrate actual video sequences as decoded after fixed and after variable-rate encoding. The figures reproduce frames separated by 1/3 sec intervals. In order to demonstrate more clearly the poor SNR in the fixed-rate coded first half of the video sequence, Figure 5.23 compares pairs of consecutive frames from the first three seconds of the video sequence. The upper pair was fixed-rate encoded, while the lower pair was variable-rate encoded. Block distortion, resulting from the rate limit, is clearly evident in the fixed-rate images. The differing subjective quality evaluations presented in Section 5.3 arise directly from this sort of difference.

Subband Coding

The organization of a subband VR codec, like the DCT VR codec, reproduces the structure illustrated in Figure 5.1. The principal difference is that encoding and decoding are each

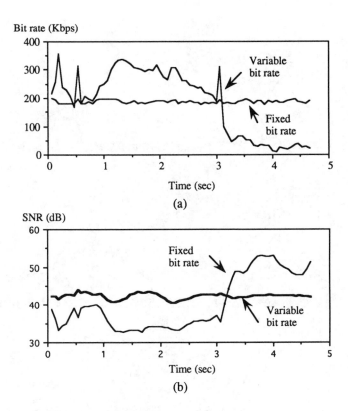

Figure 5.20 (a) Bit-rate variation and (b) SNR variation (MC + DCT).

broken out into a number of independent bands. Quality can be fixed at any desired value by adjusting the compression and quantization parameters of the encoders for each band.

If we consider quality from the point of view of the rate-distortion curve then, at any given bit rate, the quality can be maximized by distributing the bits such that distortion is constant for all bands. At least one author has analyzed in depth the problem of bit distribution [17], but most implementors of subband coders have taken the simple way out. A fixed number of bits is allocated, in advance, to each band's quantizer based on the statistical characteristics of the band's signal. In contrast, adaptive bit distribution adjusts the bit count of each band according to the power of the signal. In this case, either the decoder of each subband must also determine the bit count for inverse quantization, using the same criterion as is used by the encoder, or the bit count information must be transmitted along with the quantized signal. Therefore, the method is somewhat lacking in robustness.

Here, we will present a simple subband coding system in which the encoder breaks out the signal into 3-dimensional time and space bands and applies variable-rate encoding [18].

Figure 5.21 Fixed-rate MC + DCT-coded video sequence. (Bit rate: approximately 200 Kbps; SNR: approximately 42 dB; frames: 1/3 sec apart.)

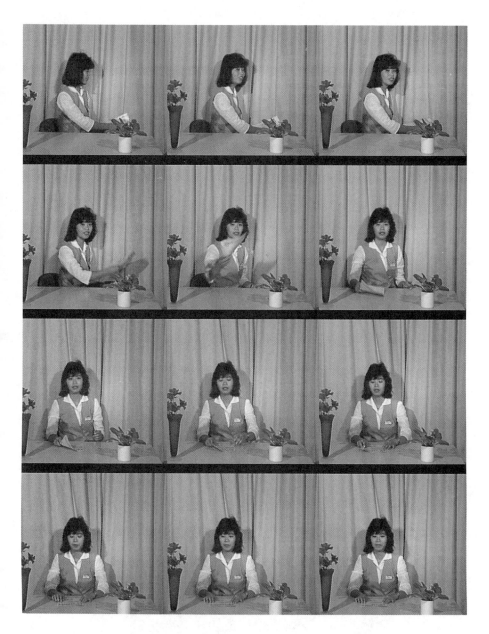

Figure 5.22 Variable-rate MC + DCT-coded video sequence. (Bit rate: approximately 200 Kbps; SNR: approximately 42 dB; frames: 1/3 sec apart.)

Figure 5.23a Comparison of coding quality for MC + DCT: fixed rate (SNR = 32.8 dB).

Figure 5.23b Comparison of coding quality for MC + DCT: variable rate (SNR = 43.3 dB).

Figure 5.24 shows a block diagram of an 11-band subband encoder. The video signal is first low- and high-pass filtered in the temporal domain. The following low-order perfect reconstruction filter is used in this step.

$$H_l = \frac{1}{2}(1 + z^{-1}) \qquad H_h = \frac{1}{2}(1 - z^{-1}) \tag{5.16}$$

Filtering in the temporal domain allows subband encoding to make use of temporal redundancy. For each temporal component, the signal is subband partitioned in the horizontal and vertical directions. Bands 1–4 are filtered twice in both the horizontal and vertical directions. For these bands, the pixel count is reduced to 1/32 that of the original signal. Bands 5–11 are filtered once in each direction; the resulting pixel counts are thus reduced by a factor of 8. The spatial subband partitioning filter uses the perfect reconstruction filter discussed in Section 5.4.1 to good effect. Compression is accomplished by applying DCPM to band 1 (referred to as the *baseband*) only. This technique was derived empirically, by viewing subbands for actual video signals. That is, observation showed that after applying low-pass transient filters in the temporal and spatial dimensions, the power and the correlations of bands other than band 1 was small, so adequate compression could be achieved by applying the simpler PCM. Run-length coding is used for entropy encoding, with two special twists: to encourage long runs of zeros, encoding is performed in the same direction as the spatial low-pass filter, and isolated nonzero values are considered to be noise, and are forced to zero. In this way the average bit rate is further reduced.

For subband coding, the quality (which is to say, the bit rate) is controlled by adjusting the quantizer bit counts of each subband.

Vector Quantization

For vector quantization, the organization differs somewhat from that of Figure 5.1. This is because VQ performs compression and encoding in a single operation, and entropy encoding can also be incorporated into the same step. Therefore, the quality-control methods used with scalar quantizers can not be used with VQ. Variable-rate vector quantizers adjust the performance of their quantizers adaptively and stepwise by directly monitoring the distortion (or a parameter that tracks distortion).

Variable-rate vector quantization can be accomplished using variable block sizes or by using multistage VQ [19, 20]. The former method utilizes the effect of block size on distortion, while the latter relies on the number of stages employed to control distortion. In either case, as the characteristics of the video signal vary locally, the distortion is held constant, by adjusting either the block size or the number of VQ stages. Here, we discuss variable-block-size VR-VQ.

Figure 5.25 shows the organization of a variable-block-size vector quantizer. This quantizer operates on 16×16, 8×8, and 4×4 blocks. The activity index, which measures

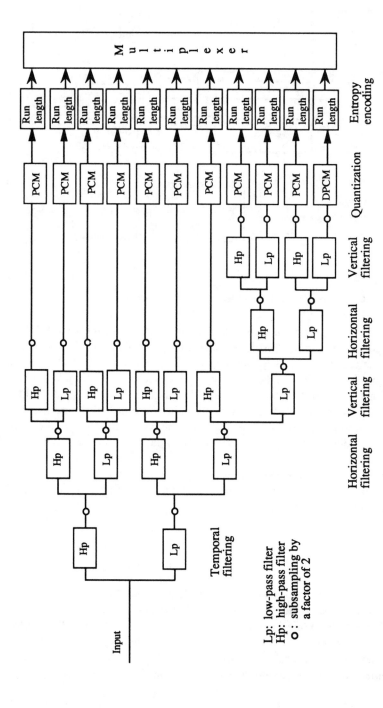

Figure 5.24 Variable-rate 3-D subband encoder (11 subbands).

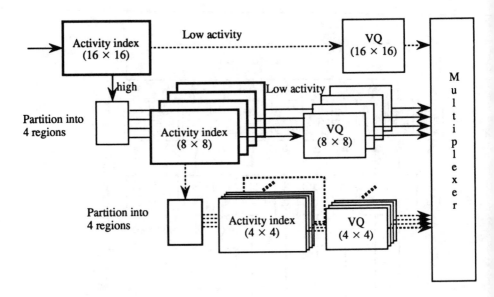

Figure 5.25 Variable-rate vector quantization codec (variable block size type).

the significance of pixels within the block, is first calculated for the 16 × 16 block size, and compared to a threshold. Blocks whose activity index is less than an established threshold value are classified as low-detail blocks, and the 16 × 16 block is encoded as a vector. Those blocks for which the activity index exceeds the threshold are classified as high-activity blocks and split into four blocks, and the procedure is repeated for each smaller block. Blocks with very large activity indices are ultimately reduced to 4 × 4 blocks, and vector-quantized. It is clear, then, that the per-pixel bit rate is lower for low-detail blocks and higher for high-detail blocks. Separate codebooks are used for each of the block sizes.

When the activity index and its threshold have been properly tuned, variable block size VQ delivers nearly constant distortion across the video image. The following is one example of a practical activity index.

$$A = \frac{1}{K}\sum_{i=1}^{K}|P(i) - M|$$ (5.17)

Here, K is the number of pixels in the block, $P(i)$ is the signal level of the ith pixel, and M is the average signal level of pixels within the block.

Clearly, altering the threshold will change the encoding quality of VR-VQ. However, the quality of VQ coding is also significantly affected by the match between the codebook being used and the input signal. Therefore, when VQ is used alone, it is more difficult than with other variable-rate coding methods to obtain fixed-quality coding. Mani et al.

[21] have reported that, while the SNR of the encoded video is affected by modification of the activity index threshold, the SNR variations that arise from variations in the nature of the video are larger. For this reason, few actual codecs attempt to accomplish variable-rate coding by controlling VQ alone.

5.5 VIDEO SYNCHRONIZATION

Video synchronization is necessary even if the video signals are transmitted through synchronous digital networks because video terminals generally work independently of the network clock. In the case of packet transmission, we have to consider, in addition, packet jitter caused by packet multiplexing. This implies that synchronization may become more difficult than with synchronous digital transmission. Therefore, video synchronization functions that consider these conditions should be introduced into VR codecs, as shown in Figure 5.1. Here, two typical techniques to maintain video synchronization between video terminals are discussed [22].

5.5.1 Technique Based on Buffer Filling Level

Figure 5.26 shows a diagram of video synchronization using the digital phase-locked-loop (D-PLL), activated by the buffer filling level at the receiving terminal. In this technique, a D-PLL controls the decoder clock so the buffer filling level maintains a certain value. There is no need to insert additional information to achieve video synchronization.

5.5.2 Technique Based on Time Stamping

This method requires the insertion of a time reference at the encoder. At the receiving terminal, the D-PLL controls the decoder clock to keep the time difference between the

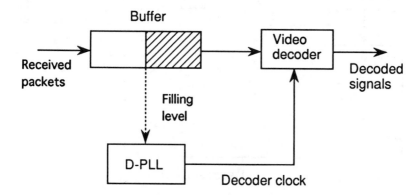

Figure 5.26 Video synchronization at decoder based on buffer filling level.

reference and actual arrival time at a constant value. The block diagram of this technique is shown in Figure 5.27.

The clock accuracy required for video synchronization will depend on video terminal specifications. For example, CRT displays generally demand an accuracy of 10% of a pixel. This means that, the clock stability required is about 10^{-4} if the number of pixels in a horizontal video line is about 1000. It is not so difficult to achieve this accuracy if we adopt D-PLL techniques [23]. Results on synchronization and dejittering of a TV decoder in ATM networks is shown in [24].

5.6 SUMMARY

In this chapter, we discussed various aspects of variable-rate video coding using both theoretical and experimental results. The technological issues associated with variable-rate video coding have been discussed, focusing on the difference between fixed- and variable-rate coding. We have seen that, when no limitations are imposed on variable-rate coding, it produces higher quality video than does fixed-rated coding at the same average bit rate. However, because an actual packet network imposes various limitations on the information that the encoder may generate and discards packets with finite probability, the quality will not necessarily be improved. Therefore, some caution must be exercised in selecting an encoding method. Those limits imposed by networks are considered in Chapter 7. We next discussed signal processing techniques for compression, control of output rate and video quality, and architecture of variable-rate coding schemes. As fundamental compression techniques, we described processing techniques based on discrete cosine transform, subband, and vector quantization. It was shown that a variable-

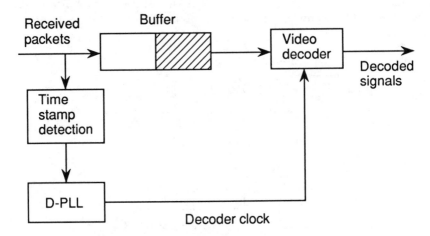

Figure 5.27 Video synchronization at decoder through time stamping.

rate coding scheme based on MC + DCT and/or subband coding is a promising technology. We have also discussed video synchronization technologies that are required to achieve packet video transmission.

REFERENCES

[1] Ohta, N., Nomura, M., and Fujii, T., "Variable-Rate Video Coding Using Motion Compensated DCT for Asynchronous Transfer Mode Networks," *Proc. ICC '88*, 1988, pp. 1257–1261.

[2] Ohta, N., Nomura, M., and Fujii, T., "Quality Based Adaptive Frame-Rate Control in Low Bit-Rate Video Coding," *PCS '88*, 12.4, 1988.

[3] Rao, K. R., and Ypi, P., *Discrete Cosine Transform*, San Diego, CA: Academic Press, Inc., 1990.

[4] LeGall, D., Gaggioni, H. and Chen, C. T., "Transmission of HDTV Signals Under 140 MBit/s Using a Subband Decomposition and Discrete Cosine Transform," *Proc. National Communication Forum*, Vol. 42, Sept. 1988.

[5] Woods, J. W. and Naveen, T., "Subband Compression of HDTV," Fourth Int. Workshop on HDTV and beyond, Session 3B, Turin, Sept. 1991.

[6] Johnston, J., "A Filter Family Design for Use in Quadrature Mirror Filter Banks," *Proc. ICASSP*, Apr. 1980, pp. 290–294.

[7] LeGall, D., and Tabatabai, A., "Subband Coding of Digital Images Using Symmetric Short Kernel Filters and Arithmetic Coding Techniques," *ICASSP '88*, 1988, pp. 761–764.

[8] Woods, J. W. (editor), *Subband Image Coding*, Norwell, MA: Kluwer Academic Publishers, 1991.

[9] Gray, A. M., "Vector Quantization," *IEEE ASSP Mag.*, Vol. 1, April 1984, pp. 4–29.

[10] Gersho, A. and Cuperman, V., "Vector Quantization: A Pattern Matching Technique for Speech Coding," *IEEE Commun. Mag.*, Vol. 21, Dec. 1983, pp. 15–21.

[11] Linde, Y., Buzo, A., and Gray, R. M., "An Algorithm for Vector Quantizer Design," *IEEE Trans. Commun.*, COM-28, 1, Jan. 1980, pp. 84–95.

[12] Huffman, D. A., "A Method for the Construction of Minimum Redundancy Codes," *Proc. IRE*, Vol. 40, No. 10, Sept. 1952, pp. 1098–1101.

[13] Huang, T. S., "Coding of Two-Tone Images," *IEEE Trans. Commun.*, COM-25, 11, Nov. 1977, pp. 1406–1424.

[14] Musman, H. G., Pirisch P., and Grallert, H. J., "Advances in Picture Coding," *Proc. IEEE*, Vol. 73, Apr. 1985.

[15] Chen, W. H., and Pratt, W. K., "Scene Adaptive Coder," *IEEE Trans. Commun.*, COM-32, 3, 1984, pp. 225–232.

[16] Okubo, S., "Video codec Standardization in CCITT Study Group XV," *Image Communication*, Vol. 1, No. 1, 1989, pp. 45–54.

[17] Darragh, J. C., and Baker, R. L., "Fixed distortion, variable-rate subband coding of images," *Proc. SPIE Conf. on Visual Communications and Image Processing '88*, 1988, pp. 979–990.

[18] Karlsson, G., and Vetterli, M., "Subband Coding of Video Signals for Packet Switching Networks," *Proc. SPIE Conf. Visual Comm. Image Processing*, 1987, pp. 446–456.

[19] Daly, E., and Hsing, T. R., "Variable Bit Rate Vector Quantization of Video Images for Packet-Switched Networks," *Proc. ICASSP*, 1988, pp. 1160–1163.

[20] Murakami, T., Itoh, A., and Asai, K., "Dynamic Multistage Vector Quantization of Images," *Electronics and Communications in Japan*, Part 1, Vol. 69, No. 3, 1986, pp. 93–101

[21] Manikopoulos, C. N., Sun, H., and Hsu, H., "Investigation of Threshold Dependence in Adaptive Vector Quantization for Image Transformation in Packet Switched Networks," *Proc., Visual Communications and Image Processing*, 1988, pp. 999–1005.

[22] Verbiest, W., Pinno, L., and Voeten, B., "Variable Bit Rate Video Coding in ATM Networks," *Visual Communications and Image Processing*, Cambridge, 1988.

[23] Verbiest, W., Pinno, L., ''A Variable Bit Rate Video codec for Asynchronous Transfer Mode Networks,'' *IEEE Journal on Selected Areas in Communications*, Vol. 7, No. 5, June 1989, pp. 761–771.

[24] Kaiser, Y., ''Synchronization and Dejittering of a Decoder in ATM Networks,'' *5th International Workshop on Packet Video*, Berlin, March 22–23, 1993.

Chapter 6

Packet Loss Protection and Recovery

6.1 INTRODUCTION

In earlier chapters we discussed the advantages, problems, and signal processing technology necessary for transmitting video signals in packets. As discussed in Chapter 2, the biggest problem in video packet transmission is to prevent the quality from degrading due to packet loss during transmission.

In this chapter we discuss a variety of techniques for counteracting video data losses caused by packet loss. As indicated in Chapter 2 (Figure 2.11), these techniques can be divided into strategies for protection (preprocessing to minimize the effect of data losses during transmission), and recovery (postprocessing to handle any data losses that do occur). These techniques can be implemented at the user, the network, or the interface level. Processing that is implemented at the user or terminal level is referred to as level 1. Similarly, level 2 refers to processing implemented in the interface between the user and the network, and level 3 refers to processing largely concerned with countering packet losses in the network. The relation between the information-loss handling level and the ATM layers is shown in Figure 6.1. This detailed diagram shows the main protection and recovery strategies used at individual ATM layers, which are classified into physical, ATM, ATM adaptation, and higher layers according to the ATM protocol reference model.

The following sections discuss in detail the application of these techniques to video signal transmission, as well as ways for combining the techniques. In particular, we focus on hierarchical coding, which takes advantage of signal processing technology in the terminal.

As mentioned in Chapter 1, digitalization of visual media is rapidly progressing. It might be worthwhile to note that similar transport techniques are also discussed in the advanced coding and transport schemes from the application side. For example, [1] is recommended to readers interested in the latest advances in digital HDTV transmission.

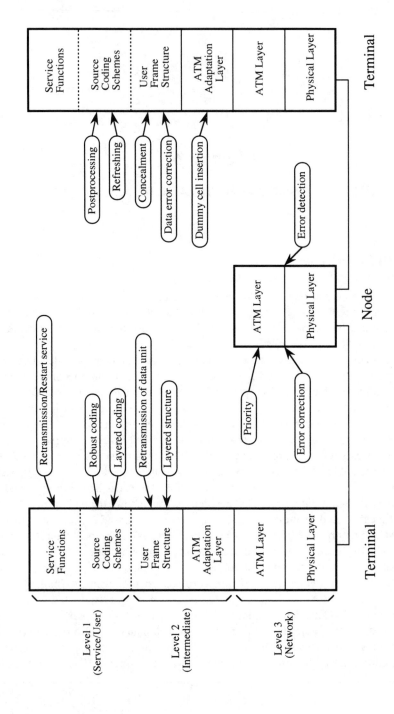

Figure 6.1 Information-loss handling levels and ATM network model.

6.2 VARIETIES OF INFORMATION LOSS IN PACKET NETWORKS

Information loss during high-speed packet switching is due to electrical/physical causes or to problems at the network level. The electrical/physical causes are manifested as random bit errors occurring along the communications route or within the equipment. These first-order bit errors may appear either in the packet header or in the data field. In ATM communications, the ATM layer identifies errors occurring in the physical layer and discards errored cells, but no provision is made for retransmission. Errors occur at the network level due to transient peaks in traffic that exceed the capacity of the network. They result in increased packet transmission delays or packet discards at network nodes. The causes and effects are summarized in Table 6.1 and explained in some detail.

6.2.1 Errors Due to Electrical or Physical Causes

The communications circuit and its attendant multiplexing and switching components can give rise to characteristic bit errors. When such an error occurs in the header of a cell or packet and the resulting address error is uncorrectable, a misdelivery will occur. This usually results in loss of the entire packet (which we call a *random loss*). When the error occurs in the data field, the damage is limited to degradation of part of the packet. Of course, if this part of the packet happens to contain vital information the effect can be quite serious, but the rate of such data losses is normally low. In fact, it is extremely low in high-speed networks based on fiber optics, certainly not exceeding 10^{-12}. (For instance, if a 150-Mbps circuit is observed over a 24-hour period and no errors are detected, the error rate is below 10^{-13}.) In terms of network design objectives, the error rate of public-

Table 6.1

Classification of Impairments Observed in Packet Transmission

Classification	Event	Causes
Packet loss (in the network)	The transmitted packet is not received at the destination terminal	Discarded due to detected errors in header
		Discarded due to congestion at network node
Packet misdelivery	The transmitted packet is received not at the destination but at another terminal (misinsertion)	Due to undetected erroneous header
Packet error	Contents of the received information are in error	Due to bit errors in information field of packet
Packet delay	The transmitted packet is received but exceeding a delay variation threshold (discarded at the receiving host)	Due to increased delays during congestion in network nodes

access networks should be set low enough that no errors will be detected during a typical measurement period. In this way, if the effect of data field errors is no greater than it is for continuous bit-rate transmission, no new types of countermeasures will be required.

6.2.2 Data Losses Due to Inadequate Network Capacity

Packets can be discarded by the network, when heavy traffic causes the buffers of network nodes to overflow, or by the receiving terminal, if packet transmission delay increases to the point that the packet arrives too late for playback on the terminal. In either case, the result is loss of data in units of packets, and occasionally a burst of packet losses will occur. We refer to any packet losses due to inadequate network capacity as *congestion loss*. Congestion loss can be higher for packet transmission than for nonpacket transmission, depending on the design of the network, and countermeasures are thus an important issue to consider, as discussed in Chapter 1.

The ability to determine that the actual rate of packet losses varies greatly according to network design and the types of services offered. In general, relatively low loss rates are expected of public-access network configurations, but private networks tolerate a wider loss rate range, depending on the purpose of the network. Public ATM systems strive for a cell loss rate of 1/10–1/100 of the bit error rate, and methods for designing such systems are available in the literature [2].

6.3 OVERVIEW OF PROTECTION AND RECOVERY TECHNIQUES

Some common techniques, such as error-correcting encoding, which is independent of the content of the signals being transmitted, scrambled transmission, and so on, can be used for minimizing the degradation due to transmission errors. These techniques do not rely on the transmission method or media and should therefore be just as applicable to high-speed ATM packet transmission as they are to traditional transmission. In this section we focus not only on these conventional techniques, but also on unique protection and recovery techniques required for high-speed packet transmission of video signals, with their stringent real-time requirements.

The most important protection and recovery techniques are summarized in Table 6.2. Here, we provide a brief description of each technique, with the exception of layered coding and priorities, which are discussed in Section 6.4.

6.3.1 Error Correction

Error Correction for Packet Headers

Effective use of error-correcting encoding can minimize packet losses by giving the packet header, which contains the address of the packet, stronger protection than the data field. We describe this in greater detail with reference to ATM.

Table 6.2
Overview of Protection and Recovery Techniques

Technique	Random Loss	Traffic-Dependent Loss	Corresponding Level Technique (Fig. 2.11, Fig. 6.2)
Protection	Error-correcting code for header information	Prioritized packet handling (selective discarding and scheduling)	3
	Structured packing of coded signals	Structured packing of coded signals	2
	Layered coding schemes and priorities	Layered coding schemes and priorities	1 + 2 + 3
	Robust coding schemes	Robust coding schemes	1
Recovery	Error correction/detection	—	2 or 3
	Replacement	Replacement	2
	Concealment and postprocessing of video signals	Concealment and postprocessing of video signals	1 or 2

The 5-byte header of an ATM cell contains data for the virtual path identifier (VPI) and virtual channel identifier (VCI) addresses. Error correction and detection codes are added to the header to protect this data. The method stipulated in [3] uses a cyclic code that corrects 1b errors and detects 2b errors.

The receiving ATM node corrects 1b errors, but if an uncorrectable error is detected, the cell is discarded. Rare cases of multiple-bit errors can be undetected and result in misdelivery of the cell to a different address. From the standpoint of the receiving party, the intruding cell is referred to as a *misinsertion* and is discarded.

Error correction technology for headers is effective at reducing cell loss due to random error. The cell loss rate can be minimized by the standardized CCITT method to about 10^{-10}, given a network bit error rate of 10^{-7}. Of course, this is the rate for individual ATM nodes. Obviously, header error correction techniques are ineffective against discarding due to congestion.

Error Correction for Whole Packets: Matrix Structuring

Cell data losses can be corrected by structuring a set of packets as a matrix and adding a parity check packet. Figure 6.2 shows such a cell matrix for the 53-byte ATM cell. On the receiving side, this can be thought of as a virtual $(N + 1) \times (M + 1)$ cell matrix. On the sending side, it is an $(N + 1) \times M$ cell matrix, with the $N + 1^{st}$ row of cells containing

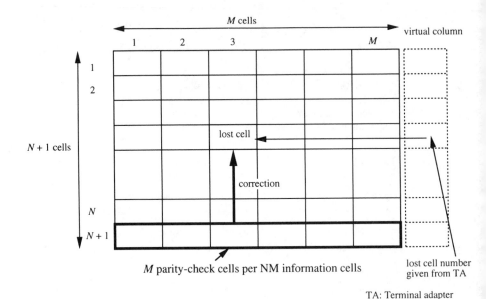

Figure 6.2 Structured cell matrix.

parity bits for checking the corresponding bits in the column direction. If the encoder inserts a sequence number into the cell adaptation layer, cell loss can be detected and the position of the lost cell or cells determined. The contents of the parity cell in the $N + 1^{st}$ row can then be used to restore the lost cell or cells, so long as no more than one cell has been lost in any column. In order to make corrections in all cases, N must be larger than the minimum cell gap produced by the cell loss, and M must be the maximum number of continuously lost cells [4].

6.3.2 Protection by Packet Priority

A natural approach is to attempt to ensure an appropriate level of quality for each service class by assigning some sort of priority to packets. The characteristics to be assured might include delay time (absolute value and variation) and the loss rate. In order to enforce a quality prioritization scheme that reflects actual demands, the multiplexing nodes must know how to handle prioritized packets whenever packets are scheduled or discarded. When scheduling, the multiplexing nodes must output high-priority packets first in order to minimize delay. When discarding, low-priority packets must be discarded first when node buffer overflow threatens [5].

This technique is useful for prioritizing a certain type of service or, within a single service, for protecting, for example, important parts of a video signal. The latter objective assumes the existence of a process that creates a hierarchical structure and inserts important data into high-priority packets. Assignment of priorities on a per-connection basis is another way of assuring the quality of a service. In this case, priority can be determined from data in the header (such as VPI/VCI). However, before such a connection request is accepted, it must be determined whether or not the network can accommodate the level of quality demanded by the service. This control function is performed by the connection admission control, an important concept in the provision of services on a packet network. Connection admission control is discussed in Section 7.2.

The actual prioritization of signals can be accomplished by hierarchical encoding technology, an exciting new field of signal processing developed for the packet transmission of video. It is discussed in detail in Section 6.4.

6.3.3 Structured Packing of Signals

Another technology for imposing hierarchy on a signal is structured packing; encoded data is packed in such a way as to localize the impact of bit errors and packet losses. As explained in Chapter 2, this is realized within the ATM framework by a construct called the ATM adaptation layer (AAL) protocol. The AAL framework has been determined, but because the contents are intimately related to service specifications, detailed standardization would, as yet, be premature. Here, we limit our discussion to the basic concept of packing.

FEC and Interleaving

In general, interleaving protects from burst errors that destroy multiple bits at one time. Combining bit interleaving with a forward error-correcting code (FEC) is a well-known and widely used technique for localizing the impact of errors. This technique is generally independent of the video encoding method, and while not always optimal for video signals, it is very widely applicable.

FEC and bit interleaving are done before the video encoding data are assembled into packets and can therefore be conceived as a part of the user framing function, as shown in Figure 6.3. A simple example of these functions can be explained as follows. The output of the source encoder is partitioned into blocks of k bits. An L bit-error-correcting code is added, creating blocks of $k + L = m$ bits. Assuming that 1B errors can be corrected, if these m-bit data blocks are interleaved in 1b units, as shown in Figure 6.4, blocks can be restored even if one cell per block has been lost. The lost cell can be identified, for example, by maintaining a sequence number (the cell identifier (CI) in the diagram).

The L-bit overhead required for this technique reduces transmission efficiency. When the error rate is low, this degree of protection is unwarranted. In the literature [6] predicts that such protection becomes necessary for a transmission rate of about 150 Mbps with an error rate around 10^{-8}.

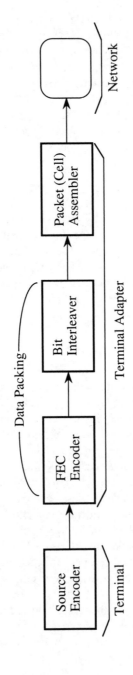

Figure 6.3 Configuration of terminal adapter (sending side).

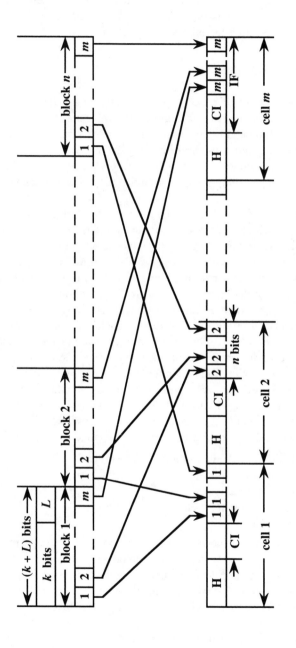

H: header, CI: cell identifier, IF: information field

Figure 6.4 Bit interleaving on FEC block and cell basis.

Similar but more complex techniques are to be adopted for the latest video transmission systems. A practical example is the Advanced Television Research Consortium's system proposal for the U.S. High-Definition TV system [7].

Structured Packing of Encoded Data

In this section we discuss methods of structuring data that take into account the characteristics of encoded video signal data. In sophisticated encoding methods, such as H.261, which is a CCITT standard method [8], an extremely complex structure is imposed. With variable-length encoding, a 1b error in part of a string can make it impossible to recover the rest of the string, so the encoded data must be structured, independent of packetizing. Therefore, the data packing technique used for packetizing should be selected to take advantage of this structure.

The layered structure of H.261 coded data is shown in Figure 6.5. H.261 is an encoding method based on motion compensation and discrete cosine transform (MC + DCT). A single video frame comprises a header and twelve groups of blocks (GOB). The GOBs comprise a maximum of 33 macro blocks (MBs). An MB corresponds to a 16 × 16 pixel block (the basic unit for motion compensation). The number of MBs varies because any MB that is judged to represent no significant motion between frames will not be sent. The video signal synchronization is established using a unique word (UW) in the video frame header and in the GOB headers. An address is also assigned to each MB so the encoded data in each MB is formally independent, but the type of quantizer and motion vector data used for motion compensation are left unstructured in the H.261 specifications. (The MPEG syntax offers a similar but more current example [9].)

When making decisions about packing methods, important considerations are: how to assure video synchronization in the face of data loss and how to localize the impact of loss of encoded data, particularly the quantizer type, motion vectors, and so on. These considerations indicate that the following basic packing method will be effective:

- Each MB unit should be packed as a unit and transmitted as one or several packets.
- The first packet in a packet transmission unit should give the absolute address of the first MB video frame contained.
- The quantizer type and absolute motion vector value should always be included in the first MB of the packet.

If these principles are followed, the impact of a packet loss can be restricted to a packet transmission unit. In other words, if something prevents a packet from being received properly, synchronization can be maintained by discarding all data until the next absolute MB address is recognized. And when the quantizer type, motion vector data, or whatever, are lost, new data is guaranteed to be present in the next packet transmission unit.

An example of this packing structure is shown in Figure 6.6. It is also possible to increase transmission efficiency by using a relative address (RA) instead of an absolute

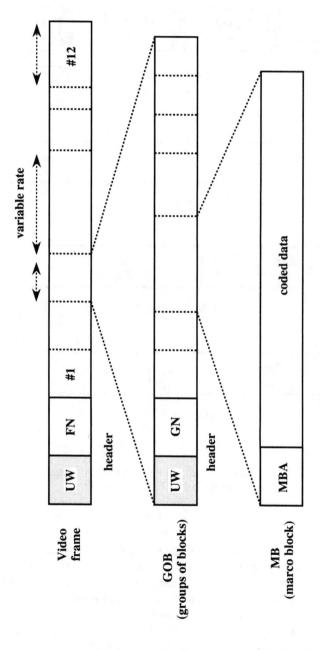

UW: unique word, FN: frame number, GN: GOB number, MBA: macro block address

Figure 6.5 Layered structure of the coded data (H.261).

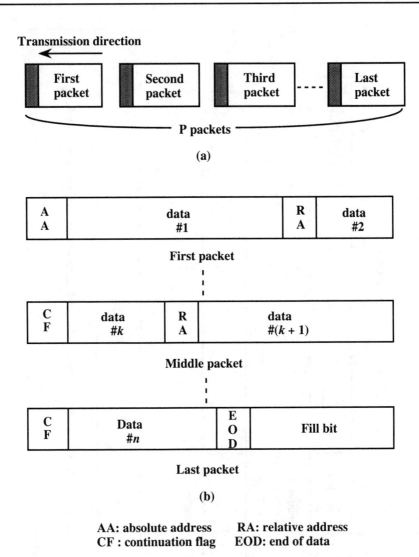

Figure 6.6 Packing structure example: (a) packet transmission unit and (b) data packing structure.

address (AA) after the first MB of the packet transmission unit. A continuation flag (CF) is added to the beginning of the data field of each packet from the second to the last packets. If the data ends in the middle of the last packet, an end-of-data (EOD) code is inserted, followed by a string of fill bits. The EOD code is useful for high-speed packet transmission because it reduces packet transmission delay time.

The transmission efficiency of this method is investigated in [10]. Transmission efficiency depends upon the packet length, length of the packet transmission unit, and the bit length of the MB (i.e., the unit of encoded data). Since the MB bit length is variable, it is more accurate to say that the transmission efficiency depends upon the nature of the video signal. The article reports an emulation of packet transmissions using the distribution of MB length for actual images encoded by H.261, in which various parameters such as transmission efficiency and the number of image blocks contained in a packet transmission unit were simulated. The packet length was taken to be the same as an ATM cell (data field = 45B). Briefly, the study showed that for transmission efficiency in the range 0.8–0.95, loss of a single packet affected an average of 7 image blocks.

More powerful protection can be implemented with structuring, at the expense of slightly lower transmission efficiency. In some of the proposed methods the motion vectors, which are the most important data, are structured, and not only current but also previous quantizer data is sent [11].

6.3.4 Robust Coding/Decoding Schemes

Since the primary objective of video compression algorithms is to eliminate redundancy in the video signal, they are generally vulnerable to information losses. Making a signal more robust is equivalent to making the coded data more redundant in some way and generally increases the transmission rate. Robust but minimally redundant schemes are therefore required to keep the transmission rate as low as possible.

The following explanation discusses fundamental techniques for robust coding/decoding schemes. We also briefly introduce transform encoding, which makes the effect of information dropouts less noticeable than is the case for DCT.

Leaky Prediction

Leaky prediction encoding is a classic example of a robust coding scheme. *Leaky prediction* refers to the technique of making the size of the prediction constant smaller than the optimal value in order to minimize error propagation. When applied to interframe predictive encoding, it results in a simple intraframe encoding if the prediction constant is set at "0." So, refreshing, which changes the mode from inter to intraframe, can also, in a broad sense, be thought of as a type of leaky prediction.

Leaky prediction always lowers the predictive gain, so it is important to consider the average bit rate of the image transmission, and the propagation of visual degradation due to packet loss, when setting the leak level. The leak is equivalent to applying the coefficient L $(0 \leq L \leq 1)$ to the multiplier in the prediction loop; $L = 1$ implies no leak, while $L = 0$ is the maximum leak value. If loss of a packet or packets results in a prediction difference D between coder and decoder, after n frames D will have be attenuated to DL^n.

Figure 6.7 demonstrates the speed of attenuation of the prediction difference D when $L = 0.9$. The size of D is given for a quantizer with a step size of 8; the frame rate

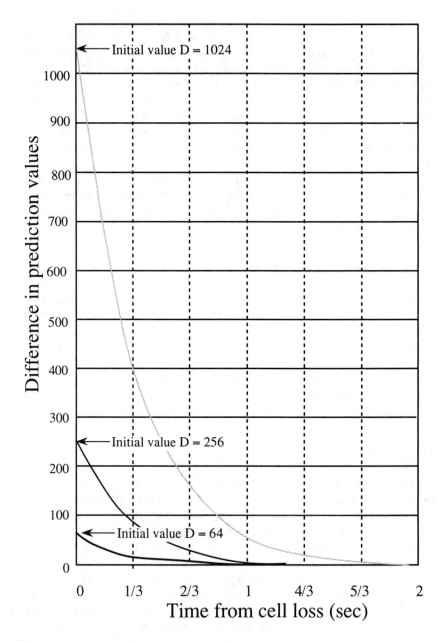

Figure 6.7 Attenuation of prediction difference. (After [12].)

is 1/30 second. The figure indicates that the effect of packet loss vanishes within about 2 sec when $L = 0.9$. This strategy gives satisfactory results so long as it does not excessively increase the coded bit rate. Figure 6.8 shows that the bit rate increases quite slowly as leakage is introduced. For the three types of video data investigated, the increase in the

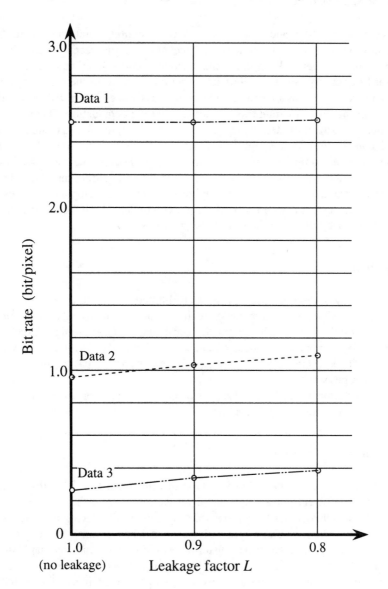

Figure 6.8 Bit-rate increase with leaky prediction. (After [12].)

bit rate is negligible [12]. (See [13] for current discussions of leaky prediction in MPEG standardization.)

Insertion of Additional Information

Error protection can be made more robust by retransmitting vital coded data, but this strategy must be combined with concealment technology at the receiving end. Here is an example of such a scheme: With interframe encoding, concealment after a packet loss is simple for low-activity (small-motion) areas, because data from the previous frame can be used. High-activity areas are generated by continuously decoding new data, so substituting data from the previous frame would not conceal the degradation. One strategy is to send a redundant packet, containing just the DC component, for blocks in areas of motion. If the DC component is crudely quantized, the increase in bit rate is small. The receiver can retrieve the DC component of lost high-activity blocks from the corresponding block in the supplemental transmission packet and use this to reconstruct the block. This does not actually prevent degradation, but playing back the DC component makes it less noticeable. (Obviously this won't work if the packet containing the DC component is also lost, but the probability of that happening is extremely low.)

Cyclic Refresh

The duration of the impact of a packet loss can be limited by switching between interframe and intraframe coding. An automatic switching technique that compares the predicted error is often used when it is important to keep coding efficiency high. Executing this switching at fixed intervals produces an encoding scheme that is robust to packet loss. For example, if the cyclic refresh is executed once a second, a packet loss is recovered from in a average of 0.5 sec.

The MPEG documents [9,13] also provide good examples for actual implementation of the concepts mentioned in this section.

Lapped Orthogonal Transform

Lapped orthogonal transform (LOT) is a type of orthogonal transform that determines the transform coefficients of a block based on data both from the block and from its neighbors. This technique has been proposed as a method of reducing the discontinuities (called block distortion) at block boundaries created when a transform such as DCT is applied to image signals [14]. Block distortion is reduced because overlapping data is used to calculate the LOT of neighboring blocks. The concept is shown in Figure 6.9. Note that, when packet loss robs the receiver of data for an image block, the visual degradation is naturally dispersed over a broader region than is the case for DCT, where

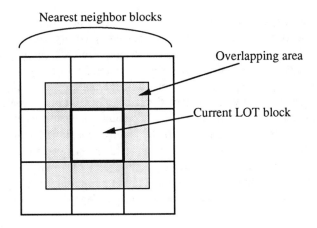

Figure 6.9 Concept of LOT.

each block is independent. Among competing robust encoding methods suitable for packet video transmissions, LOT is a serious candidate. However, since LOT is basically a transform coding like DCT, the DC component is extremely important. This component must be strongly protected, just as for DCT.

When an LOT block is lost, the corresponding block and the eight nearest-neighbor blocks will be affected. We could reconstruct the pixels in the current and eight nearest-neighbor LOT blocks by setting the lost coefficients to zero, performing an inverse LOT on the zero block using overlap from neighboring blocks when necessary, and adding the contribution of the DC component. For more details, refer to the literature on LOT recovery methods [15].

6.3.5 Recovery by the Receiver

Concealment refers to techniques for replacing erroneous sections with other data in order to minimize degradation when an uncorrectable data error or packet loss has been detected. Postprocessing during decoding can also help to make the degradation less noticeable. These techniques must be closely coordinated with the characteristics of the video signal and the coding algorithms; they therefore require various forms of cooperation between the depacketizer and decoder, or the coder and decoder. The real-time requirements of video signals make it unrealistic for the receiver to return an error message to the receiver and wait for retransmission.

Concealment by Interleaving Image Block Data

In most video coding schemes, adjacent data are highly correlated. The high degree of correlation can be utilized to conceal dropouts by replacing data with intraframe encoded data. This scheme is only effective if adjacent coded data are interleaved in such a way that encoded data for neighboring regions are placed in widely separated packets, thus minimizing the effect of bursty packet loss. For instance, in DCT coding, the packetizing would proceed not according to scanning order, but in interleaved order. If the interleaved data string is sufficiently longer than the length of the bursty packet loss, when data is restored to its original order by the receiver, the effect of packet loss is spatially dispersed. The decoder can then restore the block data contained in lost packets by using data from adjacent or closest possible blocks. If the coding scheme is hierarchical, differing concealment techniques can be used for each level. For example, missing high-priority data might be replaced with data from the adjacent block while missing low-priority data is merely set to zero. This practice is based on literature reporting that low priority levels usually contain the high-frequency DCT components, so degradation is reduced by setting to zero [4].

Coordinated Operation of Coder and Decoder

With interframe coding it is possible to use unchanged data from blocks from the corresponding position of the previous video frame. In schemes that use motion compensation, if the motion vector of a neighboring block is known, the decoder can invert it to determine which block value from the previous frame to use. This type of concealment works well for the frame immediately after the lost packet, but in subsequent frames a difference arises between prediction values in the coder and decoder, and the resulting degradation will continue until a scene change or until the signal switches over to the intraframe mode. This problem can be solved by coordinated operation of the coder and decoder. Wada has proposed a concealment technique that relies on such coordination [16]. This technique uses two principles:

- The decoder informs the coder of the video frames and blocks that have been affected by packet loss.
- The coder stores the local decoding data used for coding so that, when the decoder sends a notice of data loss, the coder can correct the local decoding data for the affected frames and blocks.

This will eliminate the difference between coder and decoder predictors. The coder can either correct local decoding data so that the affected block data is not used for coding, or can use the same type of concealment as the decoder uses for local decoding in the affected region. In this case the packet does not need to be retransmitted, so a notice of packet loss does not result in significant delay. Of course, low delays in the network should be assumed. Figure 6.10 shows an example of packet loss concealment with the coordinated operation of coder and decoder for DCT interframe encoding.

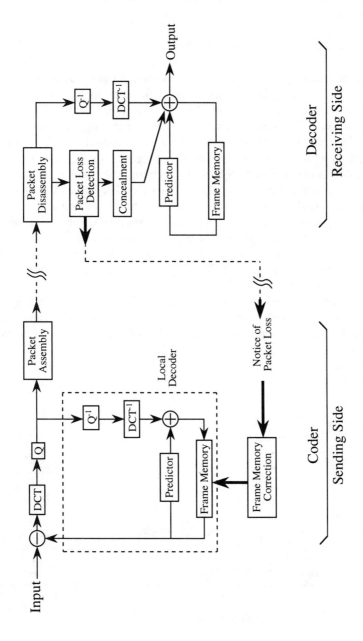

Figure 6.10 Packet loss concealment with interaction between coder and decoder.

6.4 LAYERED VIDEO CODING WITH PRIORITIZED PACKET HANDLING

6.4.1 The Meaning of Layers in Video Coding

Layered coding of video signals refers to coding techniques that partition video data into a number of layers according to the importance of the data. In fact, the term *layered coding* is actually used in two senses. One refers to a system of video services at multiple quality levels, which gives users more freedom to select the quality required for their needs. Indeed, the idea of separating video data into several categories for transmission has been proposed as a flexible video transmission service for B-ISDN [17,18]. The conceptual diagram in Figure 6.11 categorizes layers into spatial and temporal resolutions ranging from TV telephone (layer I) to HDTV (layer IV). The value of such a layering scheme lies not only in the capability of providing services at various levels of quality, but also in allowing users to select the level that will meet their needs. For instance, a user may select low bit-rate transmission if he only has a low-resolution display and wants to economize on circuit access fees. A broadcast format video service must meet the needs of a large, varied audience. A unified layering system that can be accessed at different resolutions would be especially welcome.

In its other sense, layered coding refers to a useful means of ensuring quality in network transmission. A single video source is partitioned into layers, and differing transmission qualities are established for each level. In the example shown in Figure 6.12,

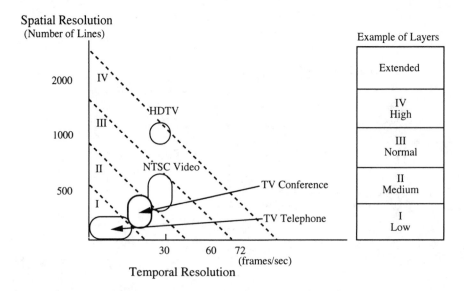

Figure 6.11 Conceptual model of layered video services.

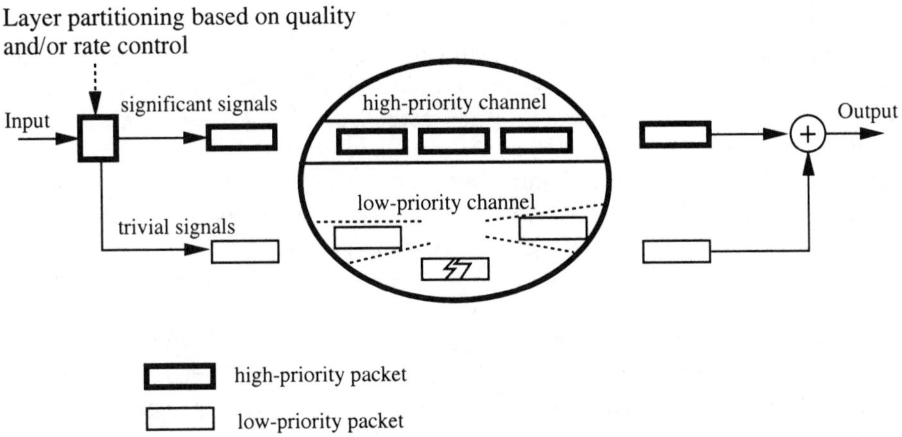

Layer partitioning based on quality
and/or rate control

Figure 6.12 Layered coding and priority.

signals of low significance are sent over a low-priority channel, while signals of high significance are sent over a high-priority channel. In this way degradation due to channel errors is minimized. This is the sense that is more relevant for packet video. Video signals are partitioned into layers, and layers are assembled into packets whose handling priority within the network reflects the significance of the data contained. This scheme can minimize the degradation of the video transmission due to network congestion.

The attractiveness of ISDN and B-ISDN as video transmission media lies in their flexibility, which makes possible services to accommodate a variety of user needs. Both the senses of layered transmission described above (increased freedom of user selection and quality assurance) contribute to the fulfillment of this promise. In turn, we have to allow some inefficiency when adopting a layered structure because we generally need more information overhead to create and handle the layers.

The discussion that follows posits a transmission network that handles packet priorities. We consider control of quality and of rate and degradation in the face of packet loss. The discussion is applicable even if the network doesn't handle priority, because the video terminal itself can use two circuits of differing quality and separately transmit high and low priority data, in order to achieve a similar effect.

6.4.2 Framework of Layering

Fundamental Approaches to Layer Partitioning

Several fundamental approaches to layering have been proposed [19]. Most approaches partition the signal based on bit planes, frequency planes, or feature planes. In bit-plane partitioning, which is the simplest, quantized data for each pixel is partitioned into bit planes (from most to least significant bit). For color video, each pixel is expressed as a combination of several color signals; partitioning can be performed to yield planes in a color space. For example, data for a single pixel can be partitioned into bit planes expressing brightness and color. These types of bit-plane layering are very general and are applicable regardless of the exact media as long as the basic data structure is the same. At the other extreme from bit-plane layering, feature-plane partitioning attempts to extract "features" with meaning to the viewer and assign them to high-priority layers. Meaningful layering approaches will thus differ according to the type of video and application. For example, in applications that attempt to identify objects, the outline of the object can be extracted and layered. For teleconferencing video, human images can be extracted and separated from the background to form a meaningful layer. Frequency-plane layering, which comes midway between bit-plane and feature-plane layering, is performed based on consideration of the characteristics of human vision; the most visually important frequencies are given high priority. In video signals the emphasis is on spatial and temporal frequencies. In this section we present a frequency-domain layering technique that is of practical significance in itself, and also as a basis for discussing layering techniques in general.

Frequency-domain layering typically assigns low-frequency components to high-priority layers and high-frequency components to low-priority layers, in accordance with the visual importance of the components. When the emphasis is on the image frequency components, subband coding is the most natural layering method. Extremely natural layering is possible for DCT coding as well, because within each block the video signal is decomposed into frequency components.

MPEG supports syntax for both spatial and frequency scalability. References [9,13] are valuable in understanding the current thinking on layering and scalability.

Criteria for Evaluating Layering

The determination to use layering will depend upon a comparison of the overhead required for layering and the extent to which layering facilitates recovery of image quality when packets are lost. The overhead includes increased complexity in the codec to implement layering, increased transmission bit rate created by the packetization for layering, and increased complexity for handling the layers within the network. The quality of recovery from degradation in the face of packet discard can be determined by measuring SNR in simulations or by subjective evaluation; it will vary depending on the layering method and packet loss characteristics.

In general, coding based on image characteristics in the frequency domain requires the least amount of processing overhead to layer. Subband coding or DCT coding are thus excellent choices. On the other hand, a layering mechanism using priority bit in packet multiplexing is to be implemented in ATM networks [20]. If this assumption follows, very little increase in complexity will be required for layered video transmission. Therefore the decision to introduce layering into ATM networks for transmitting DCT or subband-based video will be essentially governed by an analysis of the tradeoff between the increased transmission bit rate and the reduction of degradation.

From this standpoint, we focus our discussion on frequency-domain layering and consider basic techniques and actual coding rates, characteristics of degradation recovery when packets are discarded, and related topics. A coding scheme based on more than two layers can certainly be envisioned, but because ATM provides only two priorities, we restrict our discussion to two-layer coding schemes.

6.4.3 Layered Coding Based on DCT

Layered coding based on DCT has been widely investigated [21–23].

As shown in Figure 6.13, the basic concept of DCT layering is to scan DCT coefficients and assign the DC and low-frequency components to the upper, priority layer, and the other components to the lower, nonpriority layer. There are many scanning methods, with slight differences in quality [21]. For layering, the reference according to which DCT coefficients are partitioned is important. There are two basic approaches to this reference, as described below.

Quality Assurance Layering

The concept of quality assurance layering is to partition the data such that a certain level of quality is assured even if all low-priority packets are discarded. A simple example of

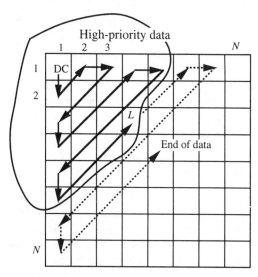

Figure 6.13 Layer partitioning of DCT coefficients.

such a scheme can be described as follows. The DCT coefficients for $N \times N$ blocks are partitioned into layers using a zig-zag scan. L of the m $(= N^2)$ DCT coefficients, including the DC components, are assigned to the high-priority layer; the remaining, higher frequency components, through the end of data, are assigned to the low-priority layer. (The final high-frequency coefficient is determined by the target SNR of the coding. Blocks with significant high-frequency content require the transmission of higher frequency component coefficients than do those without.) The quality can then be assured by, for instance, defining the SNR of the local decoder as the ratio of the power of all DCT coefficients in the block to the power of the DCT coefficients in the low-priority layer and partitioning the layers so that the SNR ratio is kept above a specified level. However, the impact of errors will propagate to subsequent frames.

Suppose that all significant DCT coefficients transmitted are also used in predictive loops for interframe coding. If a coefficient at quantization level q is lost, the error energy, including error propagation, will be $q^2(1 + a^2 + a^4 + \ldots) = q^2/(1 - a^2)$. The maximum error when all low-priority layer data is lost can be determined by summing the worst-case value for all low-priority layer coefficients. The partition between the two layers can be set to prevent this value from exceeding a certain threshold. In this way quality (as an error energy threshold) is assured even when all low-priority packets are lost.

Alternatively, we might determine not to use low-priority data for prediction, since the packet-loss probability is much higher than for high-priority data. In this scheme, errors due to the discard of low-priority packets do not propagate into subsequent frames. We can assume that almost all the low-priority data consist of high-frequency coefficients. Because high-frequency coefficients typically exhibit little interframe correlation, the efficiency of prediction will not be significantly reduced. Figure 6.14 shows interframe correlations of DCT coefficients measured for five actual video signals. Declining to use low-priority data for prediction is therefore equivalent to selectively using a leaky prediction coefficient of zero for the high-frequency components (in the low-priority layer) only.

This conceptualization suggests a generalization for DCT-based layering. Suppose that prediction were performed using an optimal prediction coefficient $a(n)$ for each DCT coefficient. If the quantization level for each DCT coefficient is expressed as $q(n)$, the total error D arising when low-priority layers are discarded is

$$D = \sum_{n=L+1}^{M} q(n)^2/[1 - a(n)^2] \qquad (6.1)$$

If data is partitioned such that D will not exceed a maximum value D_{max}, it is possible to insure a maximum error even if all low-priority-level packets are discarded. In other words, the position at which high-frequency coefficients are partitioned into low priority is chosen so that D cannot exceed D_{max}. By controlling the parameter D_{max}, which determines the worst-case quality, it is possible to control the proportion of coded data assigned high priority.

	0	1	2			7		
0	1.0	0.9	0.9	0.8	0.5			
1	0.9	0.9	0.8	0.7				
2	0.9	0.8	0.7	0.4				
	0.8	0.7	0.5					
	0.7	0.4						
	0.4	0.2						
7								

Figure 6.14 Interframe correlation of DCT coefficients. (Average values obtained from five video sources: Y signals.) (Only nonzero values are shown.)

Rate Control for Layered Coding

It is also possible to base layering on the bit rates of the high- and low-priority layers. That is, coding is controlled such that the proportion of priority data to the total amount of data (or the ratio of high- to low-priority data) is kept fixed. The maximum output over a given time period of the terminal's encoder is restricted in order to protect the network from congestion. This type of restriction is necessary in order to design a congestion-free network, but if the network handles two priorities, it would help to know the differing variability characteristics of high- and low-priority data. This raises the possibility of layering by rate control. If the network becomes so congested that it is about to begin discarding high-priority data, it could instead impose a more stringent rate control on the high-priority data; the restricted volume of high priority data would result in some degradation, but not as much as if entire packets of priority data were to be discarded. (One extreme example of rate control on high-priority data is to keep it constant. From the viewpoint of traffic management, this is a solution to layered packet video transmission as discussed in Section 7.3.)

This type of rate control is relatively simple to implement using DCT. First the rate for quantizing all the coefficients in the blocks to be coded must be calculated, and then coefficients must be partitioned into layers so that the rate of the high-priority coefficients is $R_p\%$.

In fact, the proportion of high-priority data will be about the same as when quality-based layering is performed. For practical purposes then, it is probably adequate to use quality-control-based layering under normal conditions (that is, network traffic conditions in which only low-priority data is likely to be discarded).

Congested conditions in which even high-priority data is likely to be discarded are not supposed to occur and indicate either a flawed network design or a user who is sending more data than authorized by agreement with the network. Under such conditions the network ceases to support its basic data transmission function. Terminals need not be designed to handle such situations; it is beyond their mission.

A Comparison of Video Coding Layered by Rate and by Quality

Figure 6.15 shows an example of two-layer DCT coding [21]. The DCT coefficients are partitioned into two layers and prediction uses only the high-priority data (HPD). Low-priority data (LPD) is sent as is, without prediction. The rate and quality characteristics for the layering based on rate control (method A) and on quality control (method B) are discussed below.

Method A: DCT coefficients are partitioned such that $x\%$ of all coded data in each block will be in the high-priority layer.

Method B: The total coefficient power to be coded is determined for each block, and coefficients are partitioned such that the total power of the coefficients in the high-priority layer is a fixed proportion of the total coefficient power (x dB).

Figures 6.16 and 6.17 show the results of computer simulations of layered encoding based on these methods, using actual video signals. The simulations used a packet length of 64B and an image of 720×480 pixels. Figure 6.16 shows that the layering increases the volume of coded information due to the additional data. Figure 6.18 demonstrates that the increased information volume when layering is used is due to "stuffing," which arises when unlayered bit sequences are packetized into layers. The amount of this increase varies with the proportion of high-priority data (HPD) to the total. The figure shows that the increase is broadly similar for methods A and B, with a very slight advantage to method B. The increase in method B is 5% when high-priority data accounts for 50% of the total.

Figure 6.17 shows the relation between the proportion of high-priority data and SNR when all low-priority data has been lost, a worst case scenario unlikely to be encountered in actual transmissions. This graph indicates that method B (quality control) also has a slight edge in terms of SNR. Increase in transmission bit rates due to layering is discussed in Section 6.5.

6.4.4 Layered Coding Based on Subband Partitioning

In general, adaptive control must be cognizant of the characteristics of video signals if frequency domain layering is to be optimized for the best quality. With subband partitioning, the signal is partitioned into M narrow bands ($M \geqslant 2$). Adaptive layering is performed by partitioning these bands into higher and lower priority layers according to

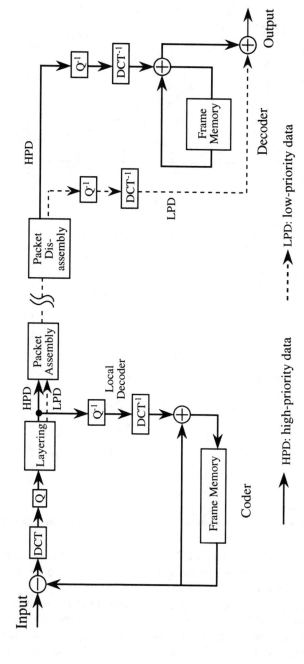

Figure 6.15 Example of two-layer DCT.

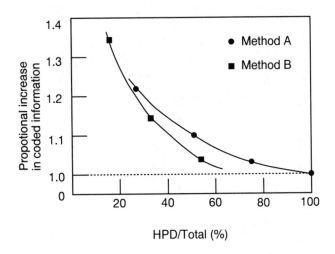

Figure 6.16 Proportional increase in coded information. (After [21].)

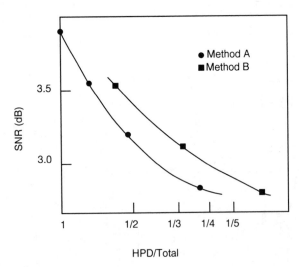

Figure 6.17 Relation between high-priority data ratio and SNR of processed picture. (After [21].)

their signal power. (In contrast, with DCT, the layering may vary for each block based on the spatial properties of the video signal.) In terms of amenability to quality-based layering, subband coding is very natural and simple [24].

When evaluating layering schemes, the important parameter to consider is the image degradation that results from loss of low-priority data. For example, in a two-layer subband format, loss of a high-frequency band will cause term $H_l(-z)X(-z)G_l(z)$ of (5.13) not to be canceled. It will thus appear as aliasing noise, and the high-frequency component term

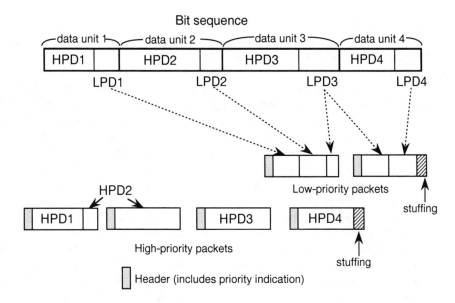

Figure 6.18 Concept of two-layered packetization.

$H_h(z)X(z)G_h(z)$ will be lost. In other words, perfect reconstruction is impossible when the low-priority layer is lost. However, unlike block distortion, the degradation will be distributed across the image frame, and thus less noticeable.

Karlsson et al. have studied packet loss under subband coding [25–27]. Their results indicate that, even if several percent of the high-frequency subband data is discarded, degradation is not observable to the naked eye. There seems to be no published research that presents *quantitative* data on the nature of distortion that appears in reconstructed video during momentary loss of low-priority data with subband coding.

6.5 VIDEO QUALITY IN A PACKET LOSS ENVIRONMENT

6.5.1 Principle Factors Affecting Image Degradation

The effects of packet loss on video transmission generally appear as noise added to the received image. In order to discuss the effect of packet loss on image quality, we must first consider the following issues:

1. The nature of the packet loss (e.g., is it continuous or isolated?)

    In general, as the rate of packet loss increases, noise and degradation also increase. However, the effect of randomly occurring packet loss differs from the effect of continuous (bursty) packet loss. When packets are lost due to network congestion and similar causes, there is likely to be an extended period of high packet loss, the effects of which cannot be adequately predicted by generalizations about random packet loss. The actual way packet-loss-related noise affects the video image is determined by the following factors.

2. The relation between packet loss and video coding data.

Important factors include the amount and type of video data lost with one packet. The amount of lost encoded data depends upon packet length and the coded bit rate. When low bit rate coded data is highly compressed and sent in large packets, the impact of packet loss can be far ranging. The type of data lost depends upon the means used to pack the encoded video data. In the MC + DCT format, for example, if all motion vectors for a frame are put into a single packet, the loss of that packet would produce very significant degradation.

3. The relation between video quality and encoded video data dropouts.

This depends principally upon the video coding scheme (interframe, intraframe, block coding). For example, losses in interframe coding will continue for a number of frames. In block coding, degradation will have a visible block form. In predictive coding schemes that operate in a horizontal direction on screen data, the degradation will appear as horizontal lines. This type of qualitative definition is simple to make, but if we attempt to discuss degradation quantitatively we find it is difficult to develop a general based simply on coding methods.

4. Factors relating to video images being transmitted.

If, for instance, packet loss affects parts of a jumbled up background, the degradation will not be very apparent. On the other hand, if the affected portion is part of a person's face, the degradation will be very noticeable. Similarly, degradation may not be noticeable in an intrinsically noisy image. Thus, the region of an image affected, the content of the image itself, and other factors determine the subjective perception of degradation created by packet loss. These factors depend greatly upon the content of the video, so it is difficult to make generalizations.

5. Factors related to coding schemes.

The effect of packet loss on image quality is, of course, a function of the coding scheme, and is especially dependent on the prediction method. Errors caused by packet loss propagate, and effects of this error propagation are a major factor both in intraframe and in interframe coding schemes. The effect is strongly dependent on the actual coding algorithm and coding bit rates.

Basic Data on Degradation Due to Packet Loss

The relation between the factors discussed above is too complex to admit simple generalizations. There is one study [28] of the basic properties of degradation due to packet loss, but the investigation is limited to PCM coding. Figure 6.19 shows the relation between mean opinion score and packet loss rate presented in that study. The packet's data field

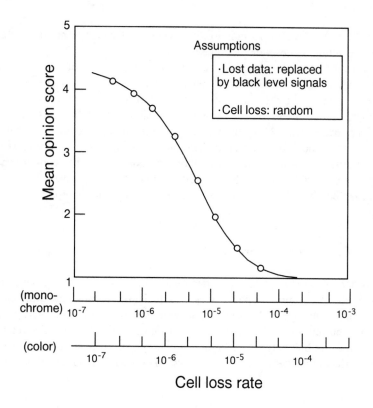

Figure 6.19 The relationship between cell loss rate and MOS in PCM coding. (After [28].)

is 48B long, and random packet loss was introduced. Lost video data was replaced by black-level signals. The mean opinion score is a subjective evaluation of video degradation obtained by comparing the degraded video against the original according to a five-point impairment rating scale and calculating the mean. (Refer to Table 6.3.) Six viewers were

Table 6.3
Subjective Test Conditions

Evaluation Method	Comparison with Original Data (8B PCM)
Rating scale	Degradation was rated according to a five-point scale Score 5: imperceptible Score 4: perceptible but not annoying Score 3: slightly annoying Score 2: annoying Score 1: very annoying

shown 640 frames on a 20-inch monitor, at a viewing distance of six times the picture height. The resulting scores were averaged.

These results provide a basis for relating MOS to the rate of random packet loss: with PCM coding, the packet loss rate must not exceed 10^{-6} if a MOS of 3.5 is to be maintained. Figure 6.19 indicates even more stringent demands on packet loss rate for color video, no doubt due to the use of black-level signals to replace lost data. Note that a MOS of 3.5 means that 90% of the viewers gave the image a score of 3 or higher and is often used as an index of acceptable video quality. If basic data is available for PCM coding, it is possible to make inferences about the quality of other coding schemes by comparing them to PCM video. However, it is difficult to generalize the above result because it may be possible to provide better quality using other appropriate concealment techniques.

6.5.2 Video Quality with Layered DCT

Let us consider a practical example of video quality in a packet loss environment in order to understand the implications of packet loss for actual video coding schemes. Our practical example examines the layered DCT coding scheme shown in Figure 6.20 and posits packet losses during the multiplexed transmission of video signals. (The quality required may be worse than for public networks.) In order to study the effect of layering, we will also evaluate the effect of packet losses when the scheme shown in Figure 6.20 is used without layering.

Coding Scheme

Our example uses DCT, with adaptive switching between intraframe and interframe coding, for compression. In this coding scheme intra and interframe prediction are calculated and compared, and whichever has the lower error rate is selected. Two-layer coding, leaky prediction, and structured packing are employed to counter the effect of packet loss. DCT coefficients are layered by partitioning the scanned coefficients as shown in Figure 6.13. Partitioning is adaptive on a block basis, assuming quality assurance layering. End-of-data code is used to indicate the partition. Certain supplemental data (intraframe/interframe flag, etc.) is added to the high-priority layer. Leaky prediction is performed as shown in Figure 6.14: interframe prediction varies depending upon the DCT coefficient. (Leaky prediction shown in Section 6.4.3 is used.) This prevents the effect of packet loss from extending across frames and does not reduce coding performance when there is no packet loss. The impact of packet loss terminates as soon as the coder switches to intraframe coding; this is the advantage of adaptive switching between intraframe and interframe coding against packet loss.

The structured packing used in this example is a special case of the method discussed in Section 6.3.3. Whenever part of the variable-length coded data is lost, subsequent coded

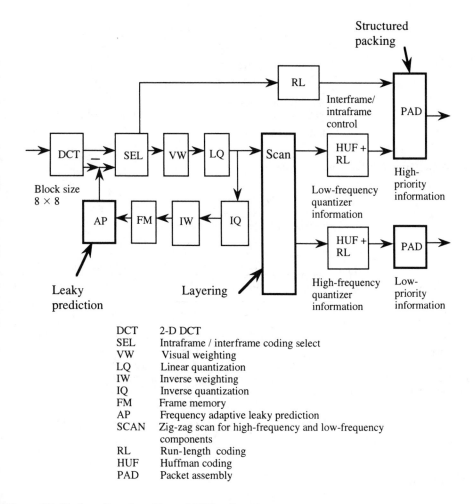

Figure 6.20 Block configuration of layered DCT coding scheme.

DCT	2-D DCT
SEL	Intraframe / interframe coding select
VW	Visual weighting
LQ	Linear quantization
IW	Inverse weighting
IQ	Inverse quantization
FM	Frame memory
AP	Frequency adaptive leaky prediction
SCAN	Zig-zag scan for high-frequency and low-frequency components
RL	Run-length coding
HUF	Huffman coding
PAD	Packet assembly

data cannot be decoded. In order to localize the effect of such packet loss, each packet can be structured separately, as shown in Figure 6.21, with the insertion of address information for the decoder. This increases the overhead of packetizing, but limits the effect on decoding of packet loss to just the actual packets that have been lost.

Table 6.4 shows the coded rate overhead as determined by simulating this layered coding scheme for actual video signals. This study did not treat header data as overhead. The maximum increase in coded bit rate was about 5%, due to the addition of stuff bits during packetization, as shown in Figure 6.21. Layering overhead is also increased by another fixed amount due to the code added to indicate the end of scan for each DCT

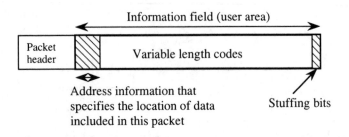

Figure 6.21 Structured data packing in packetization.

Table 6.4
Overhead of Packet Loss Protection

Video Data	Coded Bit Rate (Mbps)	Bit Rate After Packetization		Bit Rate After Layering	
		Mbps	Overhead%	Mbps	Overhead%
Data 1	4.91	5.14	4.68	5.77	17.52
Data 2	20.34	21.40	5.21	21.92	7.77
Data 3	6.92	7.36	6.39	8.10	17.05
Data 4	19.99	21.12	5.64	21.67	8.40

Overhead = (bit rate after packetization or layering—encoded bit rate)/encoded bit rate × 100 (%) (Packetization overhead excludes overhead of packet header.)

block in each layer. These factors increase the proportion of overhead when low-bit-rate video is transmitted.

The Characteristics of Packet Loss

Let us discuss a dedicated transmission system that statistically multiplexes video signals for transmission. As an example, we will consider a multiplexed video distribution system using an ATM-based optical ring network [29]. The concept is shown in Figure 6.22. The video terminals and the center for video distribution are connected to a ring network that uses a point-to-multipoint format to transmit video signals by multiplexing channels of the network. The ring network may be thought of as a LAN. The design of such a system will attempt to multiplex as many video signals as possible using available transmission capacity. For example, CATV designs will attempt to multiplex at least 50 channels. Unlike a public network design, a CATV network design may, to economize, permit a level of congestion that results in temporary increase of packet losses.

An example of congestion during the multiplexing of 50 broadcast video channels is shown in Figure 4.18 of Section 4.4, where we inferred the characteristics of video

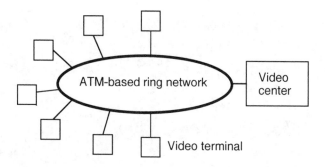

Figure 6.22 Video distribution through ATM-based ring network.

multiplexing from a simple scene change model. Although the probability of congestion occurring is low, when it does occur it results in several seconds of high-rate packet discards, with a correspondingly large impact on video quality. Our discussion in this section is based on a worst-case scenario of packet discard properties, such as that shown in Figure 4.18, for a statistically multiplexed video transmission system.

Examples of Degradation Due to Packet Loss

Let's look at an example of degradation in a video of a person speaking when 30% packet loss continues for 2 sec. Let the data field in the packets be 64B. Figure 6.23 shows, from left to right, every tenth frame (1/3 sec intervals) of the decoded video sequence without packet loss, starting at $t = 0$. Figure 6.24 shows the same video without priority handling, and Figure 6.25, with two-layer priority handling, when a 30% packet loss rate continues from $t = 1$ (sec) to $t = 3$ (sec), using the DCT coding scheme of Figure 6.20. In this case, the threshold value D_{max} is 5.

In Figure 6.24 (no priority handling) 30% of the packets have been discarded without regard to content. The block decoding method replaced the discarded data as follows:

- When the DC component or supplemental data has been lost from a DCT block, it is replaced with decoded data from the previous block.
- Losses are replaced with "0" when only block quantization data has been lost.

This does not adequately compensate for packet losses because, as is clear from Figure 6.24, once packets begin to be discarded, block distortion makes the decoded image unbearable to look at.

In contrast, it is much harder to discern the effect of packet loss in Figure 6.25 (two-layer priority packet handling), since in this case packets containing upper layer data have been preserved and the entire discard rate of 30% is absorbed by low priority packets. The difference in quality compared to Figure 6.24 is nearly undetectable. The SNR has been lowered by the packet loss, but because vital data has been preserved, degradation occurs only gradually and does not appear in obvious blocks.

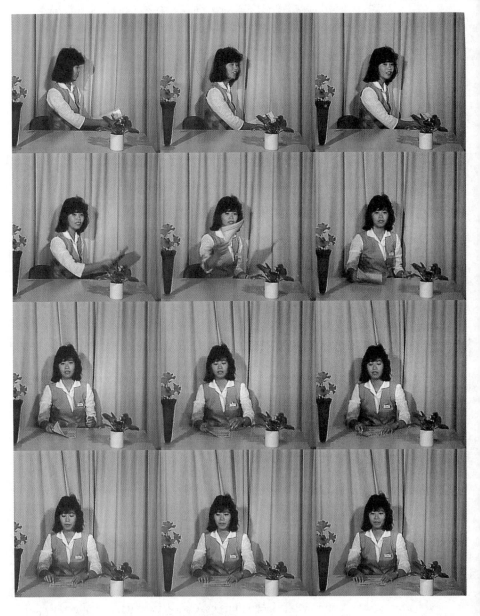

Figure 6.23 Decoded video sequence without packet loss. (Displayed every 1/3 sec.)

Figure 6.24 Decoded video sequence degraded by packet loss without packet priority handling. (Displayed every 1/3 sec.)

Figure 6.25 Decoded video sequence degraded by packet loss with priority packet handling (two layers). (Displayed every 1/3 sec.)

Next, we examine the relationship between the packet loss rate and SNR. Figure 6.26 shows this relation, under random packet loss, for two types of video data as coded by a nonpriority and a two-layer priority scheme. The value used for the average SNR was obtained by evaluating the SNR for each frame and averaging over the entire sequence. Vital data lost in the nonprioritized scheme were replaced with the decoded values from the previous frame, but the compensatory effect was almost nil when there was a lot of motion. Thus the nonprioritized scheme exhibited considerable degradation for the second data set (data 2), which featured a moving subject. The parameter D_{max} is used in the two-layer scheme to control worst-case degradation (see Section 6.4.3). Ideally, D_{max} will be determined so that the SNR degradation characteristics come as close as possible to the upper bound of the rate-distortion characteristics.

How much of the data is assigned low priority with different values of D_{max}? As for the video sequence data 1, used in Fig. 6.26, about 28, 35, and 38% of data are assigned to low-priority packets for D_{max} values of 5, 10, and 20, respectively. The ratio of low-priority data varies depending on the video content. For the video sequences shown in Table 6.4, the percentages of low-priority data ranged from 20–40% for D_{max} values from

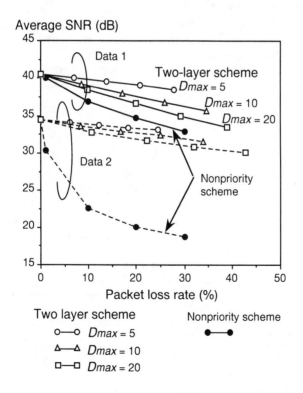

Figure 6.26 Relation between packet loss rate and average SNR (two-layer and nonpriority schemes).

5–10. Reference [30] is recommended for readers interested in MPEG-based prioritized transmission.

Results of Subjective Evaluation

An experiment was conducted in which 15 viewers subjectively evaluated the impact of packet loss using the rating system of Table 6.3. Four decoded video sequences that had suffered packet loss were compared to the corresponding intact sequences. NTSC video signals with 512×480 pixels were displayed on a 21-inch monitor and viewed from a distance of four times the picture height. Table 6.5 shows coding performance without packet loss, using the layered DCT coding scheme of Figure 6.20. The SNR performance varies with the sequences. This is because the coding scheme (Figure 6.20) adopts quality control based on visual weighting that does not always minimize the SNR value.

Figure 6.27 shows the relation between packet loss rate and subjective quality. These results indicate that for nonprioritized coding, degradation starts to become noticeable at a packet loss rate of about 0.01%. The serious degradation of video data C and D is attributed to the fact that these data contained a lot of motion. On the other hand, using two-layer prioritized coding, degradation was not noticeable until packet loss reached 10%. Layered coding and priority control are thus seen to be extremely effective means for countering the effect of packet loss.

The relation between parameter D_{max} and subjective quality shown in Figure 6.28 indicates the effectiveness of D_{max}, which controls the worst-case quality under packet discards.

6.6 SUMMARY

In this chapter we have discussed a variety of techniques for countering the effect of packet loss, one of the major problems in packet transmission of video signals. These techniques fall into three major categories: coding schemes, user framing, and network framing. In particular, the effectiveness of a technique combining DCT-based layered coding with priority control of packets was demonstrated by subjective evaluation of

Table 6.5
Coding Characteristics of Video Data

Video Data	A	B	C	D
Average bit rate (Mbps)	5.9	5.1	16.1	14.8
Maximum bit rate (Mbps)	6.4	5.9	19.5	19.9
Average SNR (dB)	38.1	37.6	28.3	29.4
Subjective quality (MOS) when no discarding has occurred	4.55	4.18	4.55	3.96

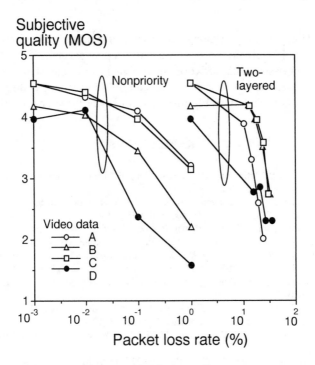

Figure 6.27 Relation between packet loss rate and subjective quality.

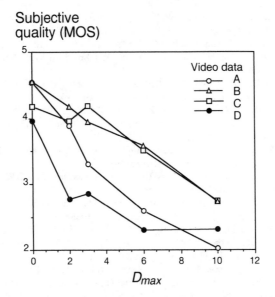

Figure 6.28 Relation between parameter D_{max} and subjective quality.

actual decoded image quality. Although not discussed in detail, subband coding is probably comparable to DCT in effectiveness as a layered coding scheme. In implementing video services on a packet-switching network, the designer must understand the characteristics of packet discards in the target network and carefully investigate coding schemes, video data structures, and packet assembly methods in light of those characteristics.

REFERENCES

[1] Special Issue on High Definition Television and Digital Video Communications, *IEEE J. on Selected Areas in Commun.*, Vol. 11, No. 1, Jan. 1993.

[2] Sato, Y., and Sato, K. I., "Evaluation of Statistical Cell Multiplexing Effects and Path Capacity Design in ATM Networks," *IEICE Trans. Commun.*, Vol. E75-B, No. 7, July 1992, pp. 642–648.

[3] CCITT Recommendation I.432, *B-ISDN User-Network Interface-Physical Layer Specification*, 1990.

[4] Kinoshita, T., Nakahashi, and Takizawa, M., "Variable Bit-Rate HDTV Coding Algorithm for ATM Environments in B-ISDN," *Proc. SPIE Conf. on Visual Communications and Image Processing '91: Visual Communication*, Nov. 1991, pp. 604–612.

[5] Hong, D., and Suda, T., "Congestion Control and Prevention in ATM Networks," *IEEE Network Magazine*, July 1991, pp. 10–16.

[6] Hessenmuller, H., "Video Signal Transmission in ATM-Based Broadband Network–Treatment of Cell Losses," *3rd Int. Workshop on Packet Video*, March 22–23, 1990.

[7] Advanced Television Research Consortium, "ADTV System Description," FCC Final Cert., Dec., Jan. 1992.

[8] Recommendations of H-series, CCITT, COM XV-R37 E (1990.8).

[9] LeGall, D., "MPEG: A Video Compression Standard for Multimedia Applications," *Commun. ACM*, Vol. 34, No. 4, Apr. 1, 1991.

[10] Wada, M., and Takishima, Y., "Structured Packing of Coded Video Signals for ATM Network," *Trans., IEICE*, B-I, Vol. J74-B-I, No. 8, Aug. 1991, pp. 609–618.

[11] Vecchietti, G., Modena, M., and Parladori, G., "ATM Network and VBR Video Source: Data Structure and Statistical Analysis of an Implemented HYBRID DCT Broadcast Video Encoder," *Proc. Globecom '91*, Dec. 1991, pp. 34–39.

[12] Hamano, T., Sakai, K., and Matsuda, K., "Cell-Loss Compensation in Variable Bit-Rate Video Coding," *Proc. Picture Coding Symposium*, Sept. 2–4, 1991, pp. 35–38.

[13] "Test Model 5," Doc. AVC-491b, Version 2, ISO-IEC/JTC1/SC29/WG11, April 1993.

[14] Malvar, H., and Staelin, H., "The LOT: Transform Coding Without Blocking Effects," *IEEE Trans. on ASSP*, Vol. 37, No. 4, April 1989, pp. 553–559.

[15] Haskell, P., and Messerschmitt, D., "Reconstructing Lost Video Data in a Lapped Orthogonal Transform Based Coder," *Proc. ICASSP '90*, 1990, pp. 1985–1988.

[16] "Selective Recovery of Video Packet Loss Using Error Concealment," *IEEE J. on Selected Areas in Communications.*, Vol. 7, No. 5, June 1989, pp. 807–814.

[17] Verbiest, W., Pinno, L., Voeten, B., "The Impact of the ATM Concept on Video Coding," *IEEE Journal on Selected Areas in Communications*, Vol. 6, No. 9, Dec. 1988.

[18] Chan, M., Princen, J., Johnson, A., and Bigger, M., "A Flexible Layering Structure for Interworking Between Video Services on the BISDN," presented at *Picture Coding Symposium*, 1.5, Sept. 1991.

[19] Zhang, Y. Q., Wu, W., Kim, K., Pickholtz, L., and Ramasastry, J., "Variable Bit-Rate Video Transmission in the Broadband ISDN Environment," *Proc. of IEEE*, Vol. 79, No. 2, Feb. 1991, pp. 214–222.

[20] CCITT Recommendation I.371, "Traffic Control and Congestion Control in B-ISDN," Geneva, 1992.

[21] Shimamura, K., Hayashi, Y., and Kishino F., "Variable-bit-rate Coding Capable of Compensating for Packet Loss," Proc. *Visual Communications and Image Processing '88*, Nov. 1988, pp. 991–998.

[22] Nomura, M., Fujii, T., and Ohta, N., "Layered Packet-Loss Protection for Variable Rate Coding Using DCT," presented at *International Workshop on Packet Video*, D7, Sept. 1988.

[23] Pereira, F., and Masera, L., "Two-Layers Constant Quality Video Coding for ATM Environments," *Proc. Visual Communications and Image Processing '90*, SPIE, Vol. 1360, 1990, pp. 1114–1125.

[24] Chiariglione, L., and Contin, L., "Two-Channel Coding for Packet Video Transmission," *Proc. ICC '88*, June, 1988, pp. 413–417.

[25] Karlsson, G., and Vetterli, M., "Subband coding of video signals for packet-switched networks," *Proc. Visual Communications and Image Processing II*, SPIE, Vol. 845, 1987, pp. 446–456.

[26] Karlsson, G., and Vetterli, M., "Packet Video and Its Integration into the Network Architecture," *IEEE J. on Selected Areas in Commun.*, Vol. 7, No. 5, June 1989, pp. 739–751.

[27] Karlsson, G., "Subband coding for packet video," Ph. D. dissertation, Dep. Elec. Eng., Columbia University, May 1989.

[28] Iai, S., and Kitawaki, N., "Video Quality Degradation by Cell Loss in ATM Networks," *NTT Review*, Vol. 4, No. 4, July 1992, pp. 52–57.

[29] Ohta, N., Nomura, M., Tokura, N., and Kikuchi, K., "Video Distribution on ATM-Based Optical Ring Networks," *ICC '90*, April 1990, pp. 976–980.

[30] Pancha, P., and Zarki, M. L., "Prioritized Transmission of Variable Bit Rate MPEG Video," *Proc. of GLOBECOM '92*, Dec. 1992, pp. 1135–1139.

Chapter 7
User/Network Interface for Packet Video

7.1 INTRODUCTION

In order to achieve packet video transmission through digital networks, users need to negotiate with the network to fix the type of service before they start transmission. The quality of the service provided by the network will be based on channel capacity provided by the network (peak or average rate, etc.) and channel characteristics (packet loss rate, packet delay distribution, etc., due to inadequate resource management in the network). On the other hand, the users must use some deterministic parameters to notify the network of the characteristics of their video signals. Furthermore, even during packet transmission, after the call has been accepted, the network will monitor the incoming packets and control the traffic, if necessary, in order to protect the network from congestion due to violations of the negotiated parameters. It is very important for the networks to provide appropriate rate-control mechanisms in order to enjoy the merits of variable-rate coding. In this chapter, we discuss user/network interface functions, taking the previously mentioned requirements into consideration. We focus on packet video transmission through ATM networks and touch on hot topics currently under discussion in ATM standardization. In this chapter, the word *cell* is used to represent the packet specified in the ATM standardization.

7.2 PACKET TRANSMISSION BY ATM NETWORKS

7.2.1 Service Categories

A public packet network is required to accommodate a wide variety of applications economically and provide subscribers with service flexibility. Therefore, the service categories that meet the variety of anticipated service requirements should be defined, and they should be differentiated in terms of quality of service (QOS) provided to the user. The QOS is defined at connection and cell levels in ATM environments. The connection-level QOS is expressed in terms of connection blocking. The blocking occurs at network nodes when sufficient bandwidth is not available to accept a new connection request. The process to accept the connection request is called *connection admission control*. The cell-level QOS is expressed by cell loss rate and cell delay variation. The basic service categories can be defined by connection-level and cell-level QOS, as shown in Table 7.1. In this table, CBR stands for constant bit rate and VBR stands for variable bit rate, respectively [1]. *Reserved* means that the network resources are reserved for the connections. Some considerations on the service categories from the application point of view are summarized below:

VBR-N: VBR, No Reserved Bandwidth Service

This service category will allow for economical variable bit rate data transmission using statistical multiplexing. The user should pay only for data successfully delivered to the destination, while the QOS in terms of cell loss and cell delay variation is not committed. This type of service is intended to meet the demands of users or applications that prefer an economical service. The user is expected to be prepared to accept and adapt to the possible network degradation due to congestion.

CBR-R: CBR, Reserved Bandwidth Service

This service will provide very high QOS, that is, very low cell loss and cell delay variation. The network will reserve network resources for these connections to ensure that the specified QOS is maintained. If there is insufficient bandwidth for the connection, the connection request will be denied or blocked. This process is called *connection admission control*. In the case of CBR, a peak rate, which is equal to the average rate, is allocated for the connection. There is no packet loss caused by congestion unless the bit rate of the connection exceeds the peak rate.

Table 7.1
Service Categories and QOS

Service Category	Quality of Service	
	Connection Blocking	Cell Loss and Cell Delay Variation
VBR, not reserved	Not committed	Not committed
CBR, reserved	Committed	Committed
VBR, reserved	Committed	Committed

As a variation of the CBR service, the burst bandwidth service can be offered. The ''burst'' means CBR transmission for a short duration. At subscription time, the user will chose from a set of peak bit rates. Before sending a burst into the network, the terminal must send a request for burst transmission and wait for confirmation. Once a burst transmission is confirmed by the network, the terminal is allowed to send the burst at its subscribed peak rate. After the completion of a burst, the terminal must send an end-of-burst signal to the network. This category of service is suitable for applications that require spontaneous transfers of large amount of data, such as high-resolution images or large files. Users of this service should pay based on the durations of the bursts.

VBR-R: VBR, Reserved Bandwidth Service

This service offers a committed cell loss rate and delay variation higher than those of the CBR-R service. The specified service bit rate of this service category will be based on traffic parameters, which consist of peak bit rate and other traffic parameters. In principle, users pay for the reserved bandwidths regardless of whether they are fully utilized. However, it will be less expensive than the CBR service due to statistical multiplexing.

7.2.2 Traffic Management Functions

The purpose of traffic management is to ensure that each of the service categories offers an adequate quality of service. Assuming that a public ATM network is available, basic procedures and functions are shown in Figure 7.1. The procedure shown in this figure consists of two phases associated with two basic functions.

The first phase is connection set-up. During this phase, a user requests a connection with a certain bandwidth. For this purpose, the user is required to notify its traffic parameters to the network. These parameters are called *traffic descriptors* in ATM standardization [2]. When establishing a connection, especially for the CBR and VBR-R services, the network will perform bandwidth allocation and decide whether the request can be accepted. The decision will be based on the notified requirements and available network resources. This function is called *connection admission control*. Bandwidth allocation management and congestion control are important topics to provide packet transmission channels that offer consistent performance in the presence of statistically varying loads on the network. Readers interested in bandwidth allocation and congestion control are recommended to read [1,3–10].

The second phase is defined as a period of packet transfer over the provided channel. In this phase, the network observes incoming packets from each user and controls the traffic to prevent violations of the agreed-upon descriptors. This control is generally called *policing*. In ATM standardization, the rate control function based on traffic descriptors and policing is called usage parameter control (UPC) [11]. There are various policing mechanisms under study along with the ATM standardization issues.

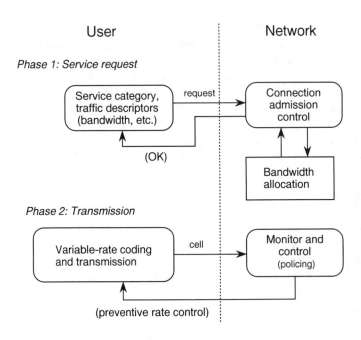

Figure 7.1 Traffic management procedures in packet networks.

In addition to these major functions, there are functions to be considered that support packet video transmission. They are related to network provisioning, congestion indication, and priority control. These functions are summarized in Table 7.2.

7.2.3 Video Transmission Based on ATM Services

The CBR-R service is equivalent to conventional fixed-rate channels and can accommodate traditional fixed-rate video transmission. On the other hand, the VBR-N service will provide variable-rate channels that match the demand of packet video transmission. The user can enjoy a cheap packet video transmission service by accepting infrequent video quality degradation due to congestion. The network can also provide a high-quality packet video transmission service based on a two-layer scheme using different categories. An example of the two-layer scheme is to use the CBR-R category as a high-priority channel and the VBR-N category as an additional information channel. This type of service assumes that connections have different priority levels assigned. The priority is called connection-level priority. Priority control is achieved, for example, by preparing two logical buffers corresponding to the two connection priority levels.

Another typical way of achieving packet video transmission using an ATM service category is to use a VBR-R category with a priority packet handling mechanism so that the user can achieve two-layer packet video transmission. The mechanism is called cell-

Table 7.2
Example of Traffic Management Functions

Service Category	Provisioning	Connection Admission Control	Usage Parameter Control	Congestion Indication	Priority Control
VBR-N	Provision network resources for different service categories	No allocation	Enforce peak rate	Inform users of potential congestion	Assign low priority to nonreserved connection; selectively discard lower priority cells first, if necessary
CBR-R	Provision network resources for different service categories	Allocate peak rate	Enforce peak rate	Not applicable	Assign high priority to reserved connection
VBR-R	Provision network resources for different service categories	Allocate bandwidth less than peak	Enforce peak rate and other parameters	Not applicable	Assign high priority to reserved connection

level priority control. Cells belonging to the same connection can be assigned different priority by using an information bit called the cell loss priority (CLP) bit [11].

Figure 7.2 summarizes these packet video service schemes.

7.3 USAGE PARAMETER CONTROL

A usage parameter control (UPC) function is required to ensure that incoming traffic does not exceed the traffic descriptor negotiated between the user and the network. The function is achieved by observing the parameters for each user and controlling incoming packets from the user based on the observation. In this section, we call this function policing.

In general, the traffic parameters should be defined deterministically and in a form that can be interpreted by the user. The policing mechanism should be simple and effective enough to ensure that violation by some users will not result in bandwidth reduction or performance degradation for other users. There are two types of policing in terms of the relationship between the video codec and the policing function, as shown in Figure 7.3. With open-loop policing, when violation is detected in a codec's traffic, packets from the codec may be discarded or tagged (assigned with low priorities). In the preventive policing,

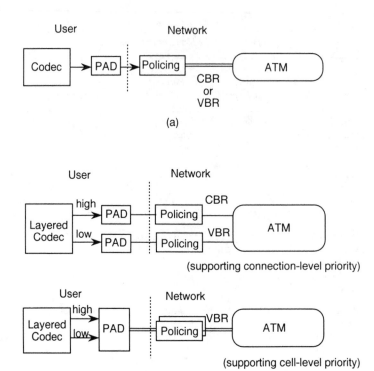

Figure 7.2 Packet video service schemes supported by ATM networks: (a) one-layer scheme and (b) two-layer scheme.

shown in Figure 7.3(b), the policing function may control the codec so that traffic will not violate the contract defined by the traffic descriptors.

In this section, we discuss UPC for packet video, focusing on traffic descriptors and policing methods.

7.3.1 Basic UPC Algorithms: Peak and Average Rate Control

For the CBR service, it is evident that the peak (or average) bit rate is an adequate traffic descriptor. In general, bandwidth allocation and policing are performed using the peak rate for CBR services. For VBR services, however, we need some additional consideration on varying the bit rate to realize statistical multiplexing gain. A conventional and simple approach is to use peak and average rates. This is a general technique because only the simple statistics of variable-rate video signals are utilized.

The peak rate can be monitored instantaneously by observing the rate for a short period. The period is expected to be much shorter than one video frame in ATM networks.

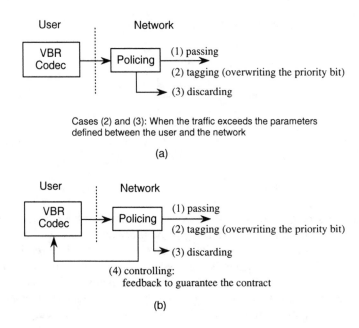

User   Network

VBR Codec → Policing → (1) passing

(2) tagging (overwriting the priority bit)

(3) discarding

Cases (2) and (3): When the traffic exceeds the parameters
defined between the user and the network

(a)

User   Network

VBR Codec → Policing → (1) passing

(2) tagging (overwriting the priority bit)

(3) discarding

(4) controlling:
feedback to guarantee the contract

(b)

Figure 7.3 Two types of policing relationships between the user and the network: (a) open loop and (b) preventive.

One candidate for definition of the peak rate is the instantaneous peak calculated from an interval between two successive cells. It is better to introduce a buffer into the codec for traffic shaping to reduce the peak rate defined previously [12]. In this section, we assume that the codec contains a traffic-shaping buffer of length corresponding to one video frame. This assumption is reasonable for general packet video applications. Cells for one frame are stored once in the buffer and transmitted with an equal time interval so that the peak rate is kept constant during one video frame.

As for the average rate, we need to determine an appropriate measuring scheme and observation interval. If the observation interval is too short, only slight bit-rate variation is allowed. On the other hand, if we measure the average bit rate over a long observation time, the response to violating traffic may be too late and the mechanism becomes complex. We discuss basic UPC algorithms hereafter.

Leaky Bucket

The leaky bucket algorithm can be represented as a single server queue with constant service time determined by the leak rate and a queue (bucket) of size K, as shown in Figure 7.4. The leaky bucket can be used to monitor the peak rate if the bucket size K is set to 1 and the leak rate is set to the peak cell rate. If K is greater than 1 and the leak

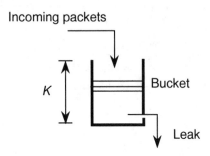

Incoming packets

K

Bucket

Leak

Figure 7.4 Leaky bucket algorithm.

rate is set to the average rate, then it can be used for policing the average cell rate and the maximum burst length. The parameters of the leaky bucket are only the bucket size and the leak rate [13]. A general description of the leaky bucket is given in [14–16]. In ATM standardization, this algorithm is regarded as a candidate for the UPC mechanism of ATM networks. However, it is reported that there are many traffic characteristics that can be admitted by the leaky bucket [17]. A safe traffic management method based on the leaky bucket that still achieves efficient statistical multiplexing is under discussion.

Sliding and Credit Window Algorithms

As shown in Figure 7.5, there are two basic algorithms using windows. A short-term average rate X can be defined as a maximum rate during a certain window. In sliding window algorithm, X is calculated from the maximum number of cells in any interval of length T. A peak rate X_0 is also defined as the instantaneous peak calculated from the number of cells in any short interval of length T_0. With credit window, the average rate is calculated from the maximum number of cells during a *fixed* time interval T. Hardware requirement of the sliding window is much larger than that of the credit window. However, the credit window has the possibility of mispolicing because it only monitors fixed reference intervals.

These algorithms do not consider video signal characteristics other than peak and average rates. This implies that careful consideration is required when we apply them as traffic descriptors for packet video applications. For example, it is reported that we should be careful in choosing window size to fully realize the advantages of VBR over CBR for packet video transmission as follows. From a perceptual point of view in MPEG-I coded video quality, the sliding window size should be at least 150 video frames according to [12]. A study on variable-rate video codecs based on H.261 standard has shown that the leaky bucket size must be quite long to achieve constant picture quality during long video programs [18].

However, a window or leaky bucket with a long monitoring interval may cause significant and long congestion. A long interval for policing will also make the hardware more complex. To solve this problem, we can use a combination of multiple windows

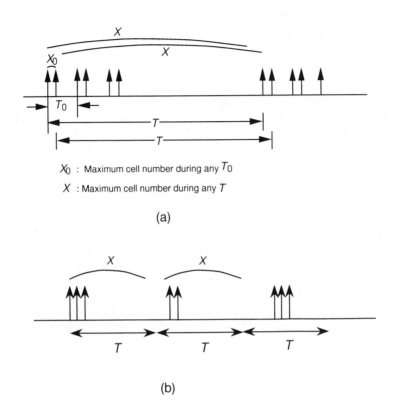

X_0 : Maximum cell number during any T_0

X : Maximum cell number during any T

(a)

(b)

Figure 7.5 (a) Sliding and (b) credit window (jumping window) algorithms.

with different lengths for policing. For example, the two-layered packet video transmission scheme shown in Figure 7.2(b) can utilize different windows for policing. A short window can be used for the high-priority virtual circuit to protect high-priority data from congestion. A long window can be used for the low-priority circuit so that we can expect the merit of variable-rate coding. It is also possible to update the window size depending on the network traffic load during the packet transfer phase. This is possible by rapidly redeclaring the usage parameters after call set-up [19]. There seems to be no significant difference between sliding window and leaky bucket methods in terms of suitability for video. As described previously, it is more important to consider combinations of techniques or more application-specific policing methods for video.

7.3.2 UPC Targeted for Video

Long-Term Distribution Parameters

As shown in Chapter 3, the long-term behavior of video signals can be characterized by the probability density function or the negative cumulative probability distribution (ncpd) function. The ncpd function gives the probability that the video traffic exceeds a certain rate. The basic idea of UPC, based on the long-term behavior, is to conservatively model the source's distribution with a mathematically defined distribution function. For example, a Gaussian distribution can be uniquely defined by its mean and standard deviation. So, mean and standard deviation can be used as traffic descriptors, if we can reserve bandwidth corresponding to the Gaussian envelope and can achieve policing to keep traffic within the envelope. However, it is difficult to police this envelope continuously from the viewpoint of complexity. In practice, we have to monitor at fixed intervals of T, a set of bit rates of the video source envelope, denoted as quantiles. The policing of the negotiated envelope at the selected quantiles results in an approximation of the Gaussian envelope by a staircase distribution denoted as the gabarit [20]. (See Figure 7.6.)

An example of achieving the policing function and implementing the function using a credit counter is shown in [21]. The policing mechanism is described as follows. A credit counter is prepared associated with each quantile. Each credit counter has a number of increment and decrement values that are related to the Gaussian distribution. Each counter is updated depending on the number of cells passed during the measurement period and evaluated. Thus, at the end of each period, the maximum time a video source is allowed to send continuously at a bit rate higher than the bit rate corresponding to the quantile is evaluated. In the next period, data that exceeds the limit can not enter the network.

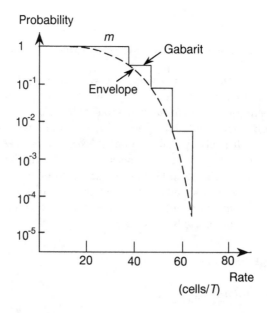

Figure 7.6 Example of envelope and gabarit.

A problem with using the distributions is that the distributions measured during time intervals within a long sequence may vary considerably. This behavior may pose a fundamental problem to any policing algorithm that tries to monitor moments of the expected long-term rate distribution.

Markov Chain Parameters

We can also model a video source as a Markov process, as described in Chapter 4. This implies that parameters associated with the Markov process can be used as traffic descriptors for packet video. Heeke [22, 23] studied the possibility of using the Markov chain parameters as traffic descriptors and proposed a policing method based on them. In the method, the user declares to the network the followings:

- The bit rate only takes one of the quantized rates (variable but piecewise constant bit rate).
- The transitions to a new rate occur only at fixed intervals following the stochastic process represented by a Markov chain.
- The holding and recurrence times of these rates follow a geometric distribution with given means.

Actual bit-rate characteristics obtained from an H.261 hardware codec showed a good fit to this assumption based on Markov chain, where eight levels of the quantized rates were used. (See Section 3.6.2.)

Heeke has proposed both bandwidth allocation and policing methods using the Markov chain parameters and their effectiveness was confirmed [22, 23]. The policing method is as follows. A video source announces that it will transmit for a fixed time interval at a given, constant rate, and that the stochastic process describing the transitions to a new permitted rate constitutes a Markov chain. The policing of the piecewise constant (and permitted) rate can be performed by any standard control device, such as a sliding window. To monitor the statistical behavior, *holding* and *recurrence times* for each constant-rate class can be used. These *times* can easily be measured by using counters and other separate control devices that monitor the counter states to check whether the measured *times* are still in accordance with their announced values; if not, cells from the source are discarded.

In his method, the policing function becomes more complex than with other methods, such as the leaky bucket, because more traffic parameters must be monitored. (When we have 8 rate classes, we have to monitor 16 parameters.) However, this method is expected to yield constant video quality and high statistical multiplexing gain.

7.4 SUMMARY

We addressed the topics of how to achieve packet video transmission services using the ATM environments currently under discussion, focusing on UPC algorithms in the user/

network interface issues. Our discussion focused on how to select traffic descriptors that can be effectively controlled both by a video codec and the network, and how to police the incoming packets to protect the networks from unexpected traffic and so eliminate the resulting congestion.

ATM networks are now regarded as the best way to support B-ISDN services. This implies that the user/network interface should be able to handle not only video but also other media. We should carefully consider that general purpose traffic management may not be appropriate for packet video transmission from the viewpoints of quality and statistical multiplexing effects.

In any event, the efficient traffic management of packet networks can be achieved by choosing appropriate traffic parameters, policing mechanisms, and bandwidth allocation, as previously mentioned. It is very important to optimize the overall performance because these three functions are very much related to each other.

REFERENCES

[1] Wernik, M., Aboul-Magd, O., and Gilbert, H., "Traffic Management for B-ISDN Services," *IEEE Network*, September 1992, pp. 10–19.

[2] Phung, V., "Selection of Traffic Descriptors," Contribution to ANSI T1S1.5, Aug. 1991.

[3] Bae, J. J., and Suda, T., "Survey of Traffic Control Schemes and Protocols in ATM Networks," *Proc. IEEE*, Vol. 79, No. 2, Feb. 1991, pp. 170–189.

[4] Hong, D., and Suda, T., "Congestion Control and Prevention in ATM Networks," *IEEE Network Magazine*, July, 1991, pp. 10–16.

[5] Garrett, M. W., and Vetterli, M., "Congestion Control Strategies for Packet Video," *Fourth International Workshop on Packet Video*, Sept. 1991.

[6] Sato, Y., and Sato, K., "Virtual Path and Link Capacity Design for ATM Networks," *IEEE J. on Sel. Areas in Commun.*, Vol. 9, No. 1, Jan. 1991, pp. 104–111.

[7] Turner, J. S., "Managing Bandwidth in ATM Networks with Bursty Traffic," *IEEE Network*, Vol. 6, No. 5, Sept. 1992, pp. 50–58.

[8] Sato, Y., and Sato, K-I, "Evaluation of Statistical Cell Multiplexing Effects and Path Capacity Design in ATM Networks," *IEICE Trans. Commun.*, Vol. E75-B, No. 7, July 1992, pp. 642–648.

[9] Garrett, M., "Contributions Toward Real-Time Services on Packet Switched Networks," Ph.D. Dissertation, Columbia University, 1993, Chapter 4.

[10] Kawashima, K., and Saito, H., "Teletraffic Issues in ATM Networks," *Computer Networks and ISDN Systems*, 20, North-Holland, 1990, pp. 369–375.

[11] CCITT Recommendation I.371, "Traffic and Congestion Control in B-ISDN," Geneva, 1992.

[12] Kawashima, M., and Tominaga, H., "A Study on VBR Video Transmission Under the Usage Parameter Control," *5th International Workshop on Packet Video*, F3, March 1993, Berlin.

[13] Kositpaiboon, R., and Phung, V., "Usage Parameter Control and Bandwidth Allocation for B-ISDN/ATM Variable Bit Rate Services," *IEEE Multimedia '90*, Nov. 1990, Bordeaux, France.

[14] Turner, J. S., "New Direction in Communications (or Which Way to the Information Age?)," *Communications Magazine*, Vol. 24, No. 10, 1986, pp. 8–15.

[15] Niestegge, G., "The 'Leaky Bucket' Policing Method in the ATM (Asynchronous Transfer Mode) Network," *Int. J. of Digital and Analog Commun. Systems*, Vol. 3, 1990, p. 188.

[16] Botto, M., Cavallero, E., and Tonietti, A., "Effectiveness of the 'Leaky Bucket' Policing Mechanism in ATM Networks," *IEEE J. on Selected Areas in Commun.* Vol. 9, No. 3, April 1991, pp. 335–342.

[17] Yamanaka, N, et al., "Usage Parameter Control and Bandwidth Allocation Methods for ATM-Based B-ISDN," *IEEE Multimedia '92*, Apr. 1992.

[18] Harasaki, H., and Yano, M, "A Study on VBR Coder Control Under Usage Parameter Control," *Fifth Int. Workshop on Packet Video*, F2.1, March 1993, Berlin, Germany.

[19] Tranchier, D. P., et al., "Fast Bandwidth Allocation in ATM Networks," *Proc. ISS '92*, A5.2, Oct. 1992, Yokohama, Japan.

[20] Prycker, M. de, "Asynchronous Transfer Mode: Solutions for Broadband ISDN," Ellis Horwood, Chichester, England, p. 225.

[21] Voeten, B., Van Der Putten, F., and Lamote, M., "Preventive Policing in Video CODECs For ATM Networks," *Fourth International Workshop on Packet Video*, Sept. 1991.

[22] Heeke, H., "Statistical Multiplexing Gain for Variable Bit Rate Video Codecs in ATM Networks," *Int. Journal of Digital and Analog Comm. Systems*, Vol. 4, 1991, pp. 261–268.

[23] Heeke, H., "A Traffic Control Algorithm for ATM Networks," *IEEE Trans. on Circuits and Systems for Video Technology*, Vol. 3, No. 3, June 1993.

Chapter 8
Conclusion

While no one can state with confidence what the communication services of the twenty-first century will look like, we can make some predictions about the technical possibilities. The rapid development of VLSI technology and consequent digitalization will facilitate media integration. The same technology will deliver ever faster, more flexible communication. Our discussion of the technological impact of packet video transmission and related technological requirements is based on these predictions. We focused on the fruit of the last five years of video signal model and signal processing research (1988–1993). This period saw great progress in video coding technology. The MPEG standard is of particular interest, and the focus of much current research. Progress is so rapid that this book can cover in detail only that work known at the time of publication. The reader with a special interest is encouraged to examine the literature for details of MPEG research cited in Chapters 4 and 7.

As for the future trend, what new forms of communication services will arise? What new forms of visual communication, including packet video, will be born? An additional volume could easily be written to cover all of the issues. Important themes to consider are the trend toward digital media, such as HDTV, which will encourage the integration of broadcast and communications; the increasing power and performance of personal computers, with resulting personal access to multimedia; and greater communication accessibility (through mobile telephones, etc.). On the other hand, the initial applications of visual communications for digital communications networks and LANs will probably be for professional use. Super-high-definition images (SHD) are one possibility. SHD images have resolutions of 2K × 2K or better and encompass digital HDTV. SHD image quality is sufficient to ensure the integration of medical, printing, and other demanding applications. VLSIs are rapidly approaching the technological level required to handle these images. What is still to come is a high-speed protocol that can transport these large data sets between computers.

In any case, when we consider the current state of computer communication and the development trends of the various technologies, it is quite easy to foresee a day in the near future when packetized video signals will connect the world, just as e-mail has already done. The technologies we have described in this book may be of even greater importance for computer communications networks, where the bandwidths are even more limited than in B-ISDN. The author hopes that this book can contribute in a small way to bringing the age of electronic visual communication closer.

About the Author

Naohisa Ohta received his B.S., M.S., and Ph.D. degrees from Tohoku University, Sendai, Japan. He is currently a senior research engineer at NTT Transmission System Laboratories. Dr. Ohta is a senior member of the IEEE and a member of the Institute of Electronic, Information, and Communications Engineers (IEICE) of Japan.

Index

The Artech House Telecommunications Library

Vinton G. Cerf, Series Editor

Transmission Performance of Evolving Telecommunications Networks, John Gruber and
  Godfrey Williams

Troposcatter Radio Links, G. Roda

UNIX Internetworking, Uday O. Pabrai

Virtual Networks: A Buyer's Guide, Daniel D. Briere

Voice Processing, Second Edition, Walt Tetschner

Voice Teletraffic System Engineering, James R. Boucher

Wireless Access and the Local Telephone Network, George Calhoun

Wireless LAN Systems, A. Santamaría and F. J. Lopez-Hernandez

Writing Disaster Recovery Plans for Telecommunications Networks and LANs, Leo A.
  Wrobel

X Window System User's Guide, Uday O. Pabrai and Hemant T. Shah

For further information on these and other Artech House titles, contact:

Artech House
685 Canton Street
Norwood, MA 01602
617-769-9750
Fax: 617-762-9230
Telex: 951-659
email: artech@world.std.com

Artech House
6 Buckingham Gate
London SW1E6JP England
+44 (0) 71-973-8077
Fax: +44 (0) 71-630-0166
Telex: 951-659